Trips and Trails, 1

**Family Camps, Short Hikes and View Roads
on the East and West Slopes of the North Cascades**

Text: E. M. Sterling
Photographs: Bob and Ira Spring
Maps: Marge Mueller

THE MOUNTAINEERS

THE MOUNTAINEERS

Organized 1906

" . . . to explore, study, preserve and enjoy the natural beauty of northwest America . . . "

First Printing, July 1967
Second Printing, August 1968
Third Printing, August 1969
Fourth Printing, August 1971
Fifth Printing, January 1973
Sixth Printing, September 1974
Seventh Printing, January 1976
Second edition, first printing, April 1978
Copyright ©1967, 1978
Manufactured in the United States of America
by Craftsman-Met Press

Published simultaneously in Canada by
Mountain Craft, Box 5232, Vancouver, B.C. V6B 4B3

Library of Congress Catalog Card No. 67-26501
ISBN 0-916890-09-0

Book design by Marge Mueller

Cover photo: Lake Tacquala (Fish Lake)—page 210

FOREWORD

Among the titles proposed for this book was **Lazy Man's Guide to Mountain Recreation,** to suggest that one need not be a daring climber or steel-muscled backwoodsman to enjoy the North Cascades and San Juans. The idea was rejected because it conjured up the tourist who rarely gets out of the car and when he does keeps one hand on the door, and the camper who stakes out a homestead in a campground and for the whole weekend never leaves the quadrilateral bounded by trailer, or motorhome, picnic table, water faucet, and privy.

The implied emphasis in the title finally chosen is on trips and trails **from** campgrounds (though many can equally well be done in a day from the city). The book is designed to lead **away** from the camp and into the woods, along the trails, and beside the rivers and saltwater waves, and up from well-traveled main roads onto lonesome roads with views and walks and things to do. Campgrounds are described, and the author surveys the theory and practice of "light camping" (as opposed to the expensive, equipment-over-burdened, mechanized variety), but the theme of the book is that while camping is good fun, it's even more fun to go snooping around.

The country covered is for everyone. Lack of outdoor experience is no barrier. Fresh from the sidewalks of New York or the tall corn of Iowa, one can enjoy these trips and trails to mountains and beaches. Nor is age a barrier. Often one hears a mother or father with small children say, "We'd like to get out, and we will when the kids are older." In fact, the average child of 2 or 3 can manage several miles a day under his own power—more with an occasional piggyback ride—and have a grand time splashing in puddles, peering at beetles.

Looked at another way, this book is an introduction. References at the end of this volume lead the more experienced traveler on trails and off-trail high routes deeper into valleys, higher on peaks, and farther along beaches. Beyond, for those who feel the call, lie mountain climbing, kayaking, bicycling, ski touring and snowshoeing, and what you will.

The Philosophy of Anti-City

Cities are necessary devices, but conveniences and pleasures fitting in a city may be nuisances or even crudities in the outback. Unfortunately, too many people fail to distinguish between city and non-city. Attracted to mountains and beaches precisely by the elemental simplicity, they insist on burdening themselves with luxuries and paraphernalia and gadgetry and noisemakers and impedimenta of the subdivision and freeway.

A refinement of taste is needed. People who like both city and back country must face up to their basic schizophrenia and separate their two lives.

The well-adjusted, thoughtful person who has completed a full self-analysis consciously **does not** carry the city into the wilds. For example, in the campground he does not abolish night by hanging a gasoline lantern to a tree, but instead enjoys the flames and coals of the campfire, enjoys the moon and stars, enjoys the darkness.

Camper-trucks and to a lesser extent trailers and motorhomes have their place. But those who seal themselves into portable subdivisions come evening or a sprinkle of rain miss the sound of the river, the brush of the wind, the smell of the trees. They leave at home the telephone and TV; the radio they have along, turned on loud to drown out the owls.

For some, the escape from the city is a chance to shed inhibitions. Sedate gentlemen, pillars of the community, do things in the hills they would never dare at home. They lash scooters to their trailers or campers, and once at the campground razz around and around like squirrels in a cage. The gutsy ones challenge the trails, sublimating frustrations of inadequate childhoods.

North Cascade Highway and Pyramid Peak

The scooter (motorized trail bike) is no worse than the automobile, and in truth is not as bad by far—two wheels less, two tons less. Cities will be better off when more people move about with a minimum of metal and fossil-fuel consumption. Scooters are also excellent for back roads, including (in Washington State) thousands of miles of tracks impassable or uncomfortable for automobiles. Scooters should be encouraged on roads and rough tracks (as well as on city streets) as a partial solution to the automobile problem.

However, it is an article of faith here that machines are inappropriate and antisocial—and above all, in **bad taste**—on traditional foot trails. The National Park Service agrees and bans scooters absolutely from paths. The U.S. Forest Service, hung up on the horns of the "multiple-use" dilemma, bars scooters from a few trails but complacently accepts them on most, and, indeed, rebuilds many to allow wheeled travel.

The philosophy of anti-city dictates that all traditional foot trails, everywhere, be closed to machinery of every kind. As the gasoline lantern pollutes night, the infernal combustion engine pollutes quiet.

An ideal might be stated that expresses the motivation of this book: when visiting the back country to camp and hike and prowl, **take along just as little of the city as you can.** Camp as light as you can. Walk as much as you can. Be as dark at night, and as quiet night and day, as you can. On road, trail, campground, be as clean as you can, carrying garbage home rather than leaving it scattered about as your "sign."

North Cascades

The creation in 1968 of the North Cascades National Park, Ross Lake and Lake Chelan National Recreation Areas, the Pasayten Wilderness, and the small additions to Glacier Peak Wilderness was an important Act by Congress to retain some of the nation's wild heritage in this corner of the country. Yet, these continue to remain critical times for the North Cascades. Big Beaver Valley, with its old growth cedars extending into the western heart of the North Cascades, and the Skagit Valley in Canada to the north are still threatened by drowning if the proposed raising of Ross Dam is not vanquished once and for all.

The bulldozer and the chainsaw have continued to chew deeper and higher into the last virgin forests. Most of the logging done under Forest Service auspices on public land is unquestioned by even the devoutest friend of trees. Some forests can reasonably be considered "surplus" to the recreation needs of this and the next generation. In some others, policies of minimum-sized, naturally shaped patch cuts, with buffers of old-growth trees left around camps and other recreational sites, provide some justification for the doctrine of "multiple-use." In many places, logging and recreation can live together—or at least the realities of political economics force a shotgun wedding.

However, The Mountaineers disagree that wilderness and scenery must invariably come second to lumber, plywood, and pulp. Certain of the heartland valleys and gentler slopes have a value only the sacrilegious would measure in dollars. (Though Mountaineers are often as ungodly as loggers, and point to the dollar potential of a tourist-and-recreation industry based on the lovely land.) The nation as a whole (which owns—as a whole—the public lands in and around the North Cascades) can easily afford to forego exploitation of the material resources in some of the few roadless and undeveloped areas yet surviving.

The roadless, undeveloped mountain and lake region between Stevens and Snoqualmie was recognized by Congress for its superlative qualities when it established the Alpine Lakes Wilderness in 1976, also directing the Forest Service to prepare a special management plan for certain of the developed lands around the wilderness core. Other roadless and undeveloped areas are currently being identified, both by the public as well as the FS—**before** they are committed to logging or roads, as had been the custom in the past. These last remnants of original America will be examined for their special qualities to decide whether they should be given permanent wilderness protection, or should remain roadless and undeveloped as "scenic" areas or something similar, or should be committed to conversion to forest products. The public can have a voice in these decisions. Within roaming radius of this volume of **Trips and Trails** are a number of such areas The Mountaineers will recommend for Wilderness; a few examples are shores and uplands of Lake Chelan; the jewel of Devil's Gulch not far from Wenatchee; inclusion of Long Draw and Long Swamp in the Pasayten Wilderness; adding areas contiguous to Glacier Peak Wilderness, such as Cascade River, Jug Lake, Meadow Creek, and Ragged Ridge; giving Grizzly Peak, just north of the Stevens Pass highway, its just due as Wilderness, as well as Boulder River, and the friendly gem of Mt. Higgins just west of Darrington.

And more, all of the Skagit River and its tributaries should finally be designated Scenic or Recreation or Wild, as appropriate, by Congress, and additions by the Washington State Legislature to further its praiseworthy action of 1977 making the Skykomish the first State Recreation River. These and others must be protected for all time as free-flowing wild, scenic, or recreation rivers from the dam-builders and the valley-flooders, the subdividers and the polluters.

San Juan Islands

Until recently, this unique archipelago seemed outside the turbulent 20th-century continuum, permanently safe.

Today, Fidalgo Island, largely a "farm" of oil refinery tanks and stacks, is the destination of ever more and ever larger tankers full of oil, threading their way through the narrow passages of the San Juans—with the constant threat of even just one spill, a spill that can smother with oil the beaches, the inter-tidal starfish, anemones, and other tidal pool life, as well as the unsuspecting fish and water-birds.

Guemes Island barely escaped instant industrialization, and other islands are coming under the gun for industrial development, real estate promotion, and other contributors to the Gross National Product.

Some land has been set aside by the state and federal governments for recreation and scenic protection. The Mountaineers take special pride in Moran State Park, established a half-century ago through the efforts of its members. More recent are the San Juan National Historical Park and the San Juan Wilderness, the latter encompassing "bird" rocks scattered offshore from the major islands. However, not enough of the San Juans have legal protection sufficient to guarantee perpetuation of their special charm, even if Cypress Island does make it as a State Natural Area Preserve.

About The Mountaineers

The Mountaineers, with groups based in Seattle, Everett, Tacoma, and Olympia, invite the membership of all lovers of outdoor life who sympathize with the purposes of the organization and wish to share in its activities.

The above brief and partial summary of Mountaineer concerns in the North Cascades and San Juans (in other areas are other concerns) suggests the importance of the club role in conservation education and action. If you share these concerns, your membership is particularly desired and needed.

Preservation, though, is only one side of the coin; the other is using and enjoying the back country.

The Mountaineers sponsor a year-round program of climbing, hiking, camping, ski-touring, and snowshoeing. Hundreds of outings are scheduled each year, ranging from single-day walks to trips lasting 2 weeks or more. On a typical weekend as many as 20 or 30 excursions may be offered, from ocean beaches to the summit of Mount Rainier. In addition, members engage in countless privately-organized trips of all kinds; perhaps a major value in belonging to an outdoor organization (The Mountaineers or any other) is the opportunity to meet other people with similar interests, to make new friends.

For further information on club activities and how to join, write The Mountaineers, 719 Pike St., Seattle, Washington 98101.

January 1978

HARVEY MANNING
and
POLLY DYER

INTRODUCTION

If the following pages have any single message, it's this: camping has very little to do with campgrounds. Not that campgrounds aren't important. They are. Camping starts there and campgrounds in every mountain, park, and seashore area are described here. But the essence of camping lies completely outside the campground and has nothing to do with erecting tents, washing dishes, chopping wood, or lugging water from creeks.

Fun is the keynote of camping. And it's to be found along trails and logging roads in flowers, stars, waterfalls, vistas, seashells, and beautiful rocks. It's in the thrill of seeing, touching, and hearing the surprises of nature.

We make no pretense of having listed everything of interest or beauty near campgrounds in the islands and North Cascades. It would be impossible to do so. Every trail and logging road holds some secret. We offer, rather, an introduction, a sampling of what's to be found.

We hope, simply, that readers who have not camped before may find reason here to start, that those who have camped but confined their camping to campgrounds will be encouraged to explore around them, and that longtime campers who have already savored the secrets of the area's wildness will find a few flavors still missed.

Many of the pleasures here must be walked for. A few lie at the edge of a car door. But the majority can be enjoyed only on trails that wind along rivers, through deep forests, and across high, alpine meadows.

Almost all of the hikes are confined to 2 miles or less, one way, and at 2 miles an hour—an average rate for mountain travel—should be completed in 2 to 3 hours. Add time, of course, to enjoy what is hiked in to see. Readers new to wildland walking should allow even more time. It's always better to have an extra hour left than to force a family into a grinding effort to keep ahead of a clock.

All the trails described should normally be easy to find and stay on. Most are clearly marked and signed. Rock cairns and blazes must be followed on only a few. No goal here demands cross-country hiking. A novice, however, should turn back any time he feels the route unsafe or obscure.

Families will not have to buy any new equipment to do the hiking trips. Sturdy shoes make walking more enjoyable. Forest trails are often a constant repetition of mud, roots, and rocks, interlaced with patches of snow, creeks without bridges, windfalls and rain-sopped brush. (And that's the way they should be. Sidewalks belong in cities.) Tennis shoes, however, will suffice for test trips, if nothing better is available. But once a family has decided on hiking as a camping way-of-life, hiking boots with rubber-lug soles purchased from a mountaineering equipment store are a wise investment. Often such shoes, particularly for children, can be purchased used.

Hikers should always carry what The Mountaineers consider the "Ten Essentials"—sunglasses, knife, matches, firestarter, first aid kit, flashlight, compass, a map, extra clothing (particularly if you start out in shorts and T-shirt and head for high altitudes), and extra food—all carried in a rucksack "just in case."

Some of the short trails offer opportunities for "test" backpacks. Families can shake down equipment and practice the required packing discipline without risking the cost of failure on a longer trip.

Logging roads are exactly what the name implies: roads designed, built, and used for logging operation. They are often rough, steep, muddy, narrow, and dusty. Many switchback endlessly. Some seem penciled on cliffs. Occasionally one may be blocked by snow, slides, or fallen trees. (And this, too, is the way it should be. Highways also are for cities.) But all can be driven safely, with care and caution, albeit in low gear, by a passenger car. Providing, of course, drivers realize they may be forced to turn back by conditions no one can control.

A blocked road, however, need not ruin a trip. One can always park and walk. A short hike often can salvage a tremendous view that would otherwise be missed.

High-altitude roads may remain closed by snow until late summer. When planning high trips through early July, it is wise to telephone ranger stations in advance for a road report.

Campsites here range from those in highly developed—and over-crowded—campgrounds on main thoroughfares to primitive, undeveloped, and uncrowded spots along remote logging roads.

All formal campgrounds offer the camping basics of a parking space, tables, firepits, toilet facilities, and water from a well, creek, or lake. Fee camps provide piped water and restrooms, as extras. The fee, however, also buys crowds.

In the National Forests—and in National Forests **only**—one may pitch camp any place. The practice is starting to cause concern as the number of people and sanitation problems grow. But it's still allowed providing the camper carries ax, shovel, and bucket for fire control.

Firewood is provided in some National Forest camps. Otherwise it must be rustled alongside mountain roads—away from camp. More sensibly, use a gas stove.

Equipment

A weekend camping trip takes very little equipment. A few pots and pans, a stove, sleeping bags, and a shelter of some sort will more than get the job done. Many novices, however, so overwhelm themselves with elaborate tents, chairs, lanterns, cushions, cots, mattresses, tables, ice chests, jugs, heaters, and even sinks they spend most of their time doing nothing but loading and unloading gear.

A new camper should buy nothing until he is certain he needs it—and probably not then. Avoid mistakes by borrowing or renting to start, buying only after you've either tried out equipment or seen others use it under campground conditions.

There are no secrets to acquiring good equipment. Deal with a reputable store—preferably one dealing in mountaineering equipment. Buy standard brands at standard prices, avoiding big promotions and "sales" unless you **know** the gear is good. When in doubt, talk to other campers.

Sleeping bags filled with 3 to 4 pounds of synthetic fiber seem most popular at present. Durability of the outer covering appears to pose the biggest choice factor. Down-filled bags are favored by many, but unless a family expects to do extensive backpacking the lighter weight is seldom worth the much higher price.

Mattresses range from lightweight plastic- or rubber-foam pads to conventional air mattresses. The pads range in thickness from an inch or less to 4 to 6 inches, with the thinner ones favored by all except comfort-demanding car campers. Fabric air mattresses are more durable than the purely plastic ones.

A **camp stove** has become virtually indispensable as the supply of firewood in and around campgrounds diminishes. Never base meal plans on a campfire alone. The two-burner pump-type stoves are popular. But the compact backpacker-types offered at mountaineer, alpine, and recreational equipment stores are much preferred by many.

The **tent** is the most expensive item in a camping outfit and perhaps the least essential. Actually, all the average camper does there is sleep. Many campers find plastic tarps sufficient protection and use nothing else. Most campers, however, eventually end up with a tent for the sake of privacy in crowded areas, and as protection from wind in higher camps.

Tents come in all shapes and sizes. Again, buy what you want from a reputable equipment store after considering such matters as ease in setting it up, size, stability in the wind, weight, bulk, and, of course, price.

Other equipment such as tarps, lanterns, ice chests, gas and water cans, ovens, chairs, axes and saws, etc., should be purchased only after the need arises—if

Camping at Douglas Fir Campground near Mount Baker

then. All campers carry some extras. But the competency of the camper and the amount of time he spends away from his equipment enjoying "camping" invariably can be measured by how few.

Pots, Pans, and Menus

Wives face the most difficult equipment-paring job of all. City-type cooking takes all sorts of equipment, as any household kitchen proves. Obviously, it can't all be hauled to camp. Picking the right items can certainly be difficult. But the wife who wants to partake in the pleasures of camping—and cooking and dishwashing do not qualify—will get the job done. Experienced camping wives have done it. A novice will find a way.

First of all, families have no right to expect fancy meals in the woods—even if they may get them. Whims of the city should be left there. Finicky children should be ignored. The desires of the cook come first. And no family should go camping just to eat, anyway.

Simple menus, preplanned and packaged, can reduce cookery and equipment to a minimum. Many wives serve the same camp meals trip in and trip out—and on paper plates too. After all, weekend camping involves only 4 meals out of the week's total of 21. The family can complain while it's home.

Select pots and pans to fit menu needs, leaving home those not needed. Camping wives generally prefer a separate set of utensils, primarily because it's impossible to keep camping pots scoured to kitchen standards. Cooking kits are popular, but many wives use home discards and let it go at that.

Cooking aids and staple stocks should also be chosen carefully and pared relentlessly. Brass scouring pads, cheese cloth dishtowels (they dry rapidly), fire starters, mitten potholders, can openers, a jack-knife, tongs, and a couple of spoons are included in most cooking sets. Food staples should be transferred to plastic containers to save space and provide some control over items carried. Cardboard boxes get wet and glass breaks.

Clothing

Weekend trips demand very few clothes. In most instances, the ones worn from home will do. Except for rain gear, swim suits, and sweaters for chill evenings, many families carry just one set of extra clothing hoping that only one child falls in the creek.

Exceptions, of course, must be made for all wives. They suffer universally from the cold and should be permitted to take all sorts of uncamp-like extras for the privilege of having them along in the first place.

There are no camping style standards—yet. Comfort's the only rule.

Packing

A firm plan for packing and loading equipment can save time and sooth nerves on any camping trip. Each piece of equipment should be stored in the same container in the same place and loaded into the same spot in the car on each trip.

Campers use every type of container from wicker baskets, through packboards to cardboard boxes (not preferred). Check lists help.

Courtesy

There was a time when men could do as they wanted in the campgrounds and mountain trails of the Pacific Northwest. But not anymore. There are too many people now. Each person must bend a little to the needs of those around him. Courtesy is no longer a nicety. It's imperative.

Radios. Music is lovely and news is interesting but served secondhand in a crowded campground both are a plague. If radio owners have a universal failing beside their choice of music (I like mine, but hate yours) it's their complete indifference to how far their sound penetrates a campground at night. No radio should be played after 10 p.m., a traditional camp bedtime. And the sound at other hours should not exude beyond the radio-owner's own campsite.

Lanterns. Light your own world but not that of others in the campground. Remember, the lantern that hisses and glares over your camp table also glares and hisses through the walls of **every** nearby tent. Lanterns are completely unnecessary on long, late summer evenings. But if you feel you must use one, shield its glare.

Scooters. Scooters have a place . . . somewhere. But it most certainly is **not** in a campground. And campers should have no qualms about seeking their ouster whenever they appear. Scooters are banned by regulation in **all** campgrounds. But it's up to campers to see the rules are enforced. Therefore, anytime—ANYTIME—scooters appear, report them promptly to rangers. Rangers can't control them without your help. They will welcome your complaint.

Thunder Creek Trail

Shaggy Mane (Coprinus comatus) mushroom near Baker Lake

Garbage. Not too long ago, campers and hikers were advised to bury and burn their garbage. Some publications still advise it. But don't. Garbage nowadays either should be put in a garbage can or else lugged home and disposed of there. Even in remote trail areas, campers must not drop, hide, bury, or burn their trash. **Haul all trash back.**

Trees. If firewood is not supplied in a campground, do **not** chop your own. Many campgrounds look as if they had undergone an artillery barrage, with every tree and shrub splintered and mangled by hatchets and saws. If you must have firewood, seek it amidst the windfallen limbs and snags of logging roads. Some campers haul dry wood from home.

Vandals. There is little use in urging campers to refrain from destroying campground facilities and equipment. Those who perform such acts are beyond urging. Report any vandalism you witness to authorities. Let them impose whatever punishment the law affords.

Fire. Every year rangers battle blazes caused by campers who simply fail to think. In formal campgrounds, confine fire to established firepits. In primitive areas, douse all fires until the coals **feel** cool, and carry a shovel, ax, and bucket at all times.

E. M. STERLING

Hummingbird nest near Snoqualmie Pass

ACKNOWLEDGMENTS

Anyone who compiles a book like this must first be grateful for the overwhelming beneficence of Washington State's vast outdoors. Material here needed only be found; its creation was already complete.

But one still owes huge obligations to men. The book could never have been completed without the encouragement and continual assistance of wives—or in Marge's case—a husband. It could not have been written without them.

Gratitude is also due the officials of national parks, national forests and state parks with special appreciation to rangers and members of their staffs. All contributed generously of their time to point out features.

And finally, thanks must be extended to Harvey Manning, the late Jack Hazle, Tom Miller, and the other members of the Literary Fund Committee for their help, encouragement, and many suggestions.

Nor do we limit our thanks to only these. Every person who ever roamed the mountains and beaches of the state in search of re-creation also had a hand. For it is because of them that many of the wild spectacles of our area still exist today. As it will have been because of all of you—our readers—if they exist tomorrow.

E. M. STERLING
BOB AND IRA SPRING
MARGE MUELLER

EXPLANATION OF SYMBOLS

Trails suitable for children up to 8. Easy and safe walking for all ages.

Difficult trails. Safe if walked sanely and knowledgeably. But no place for uncontrolled youngsters (of any age) or persons who tire easily. Hike only in lug-soled shoes.

Sunday-driver type roads. Mostly paved or well-graded gravel. Roads that can be driven easily by the most wary driver—young or old. Easy on new cars.

Rough roads. Often extremely dusty on hot days and slick after rains. But none are unsafe (see introduction) providing they are driven with constant care. On some, 10 miles an hour is speeding.

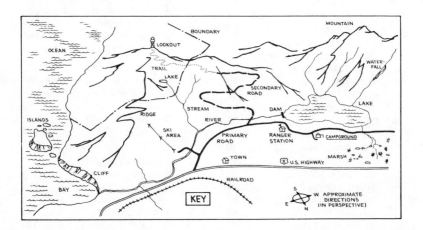

CONTENTS

Page   Page

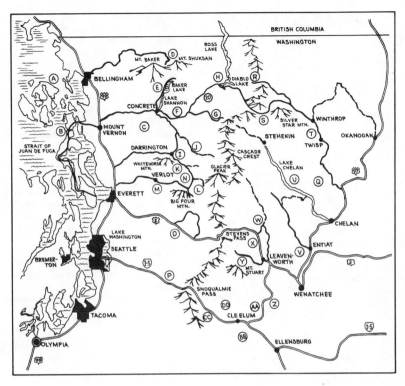

A   MORAN STATE PARK

Sweeping marine views and fresh-water lakes in the middle of the spectacular San Juan Islands. But, oddly, no saltwater facilities at all.

Take a Washington State Ferry from Anacortes to Orcas Island (the ferry trip alone is worth the effort) or stop over en route to Vancouver Island. The park is open all year round. Busiest on weekends but seldom crowded except on holidays. Most campers stay several days because of the ferry costs.

Park offerings include four mountain lakes, viewpoints atop Mount Constitution (2409) and from the Little Summit Lookout (2039)—both reached by road—miles of pleasant forest trails, waterfalls, and deer around almost every corner. (No poisonous snakes and no bears.) Supervised swimming on Cascade Lake.

MOUNT CONSTITUTION

Views to almost everywhere from the highest point in one of the most scenic marine areas in the world.

Climb to the top of the fort-like tower or simply stand on ground-level viewpoints to see a vista that sweeps from Vancouver Island to Garibaldi in British Columbia, past Baker to Rainier and over all of the islands in the San Juan group to the Olympics, Victoria, and beyond.

Road closed at night.

CAMPGROUNDS

North End—50 sites above the road on a wooded slope. Beach area and recreation center across the road on Cascade Lake. A pleasant shaded area. Restroom. Piped water. State fee.

Midway—57 sites on both sides of the road beyond the recreation center area. About 17 sites near the lake. Some on the lake. Others on wooded loops above the road. Two restrooms. Piped water. Fee.

South End—17 sites in an open wooded area near the water on the south end of Cascade Lake. The oldest site on the lake and one of the most popular. Generally full. Restroom. Cooking shelter. Piped water. Fee.

Mountain Lake—18 sites on a small peninsula on Mountain Lake. Primarily used by fishermen but a quiet camp away from highway noise. No swimming in the reservoir lake. Restroom and pit toilets. Piped water. Fee.

Cold Springs—A picnic spot in an isolated timber area. Capped spring in a rustic pavilion. Cooking shelter. Pit toilets. Spring water.

Note: Campgrounds are often full during peak summer periods. If "campground full" warnings are posted at the Anacortes ferry terminal, campers are urged to turn back. Some campers on some weekends have had to return home because no spaces were available.

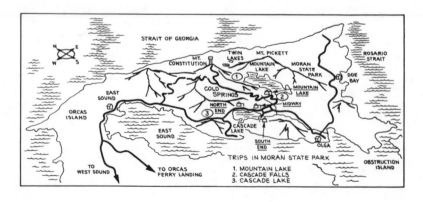

TRIPS IN MORAN STATE PARK
1. MOUNTAIN LAKE
2. CASCADE FALLS
3. CASCADE LAKE

Straits of Georgia from Mount Constitution

Mountain Lake and Rosario Strait from Mount Constitution

1   MOUNTAIN LAKE

MOUNTAIN LAKE TRAIL

Hike from the top of Mount Constitution through forest, along a rocky ledge, and past Twin Lakes to the Mountain Lake Campground. 3.6 miles.

The trail drops sharply off the far side of the turnaround loop below the tower area along ledges of lichen- and moss-covered rock with occasional views. At the first trail junction, 1.1 miles, keep right.

At the second junction, keep right and downhill again.

From Twin Lakes (see Twin Lakes Trail) continue downhill another 2.1 miles to Mountain Lake Campground.

LITTLE SUMMIT LOOKOUT TRAIL

From viewpoint to viewpoint with even more views in between.

Hike 2.2 miles from the tower area on Mount Constitution down to Little Summit Lookout (2039). Find trail along the left side of the TV transmitter building, dropping at the start through timber, to a series of view ledges. Timber along the trail has been attacked by blister rust.

Junction in 1 mile with Cold Springs trail. Keep left. A few more views in the last ½ mile. Watch for trail marker in the last .2 mile, making sure to turn uphill, to the right, at a junction with a trail that leads downhill sharply.

Trail ends near the road. Turn back uphill to 40-foot lookout tower.

TWIN LAKE TRAIL

An easy trail wanders along Mountain Lake and then up a cool, shallow valley to two much smaller mountain lakes. 2.1 miles.

Hike north out of the Mountain Lake Campground about 1.3 miles, turning away from the lake at the junction beyond the second creek. Trail follows a small stream through alder brakes in an old homestead area—watch for signs of tumbledown cabins—to a second junction only a few yards from the first lake.

AROUND-THE-LAKE TRAIL

A pleasant water-grade trail all the way around Mountain Lake. About 4 miles, round trip.

For a clockwise hike, take the trail north out of the Mountain Lake Campground, keeping right at the junction with the Twin Lakes trail. Trail drops below a dam to a footbridge at the south end of the lake. Turn right beyond the bridge to return to camp.

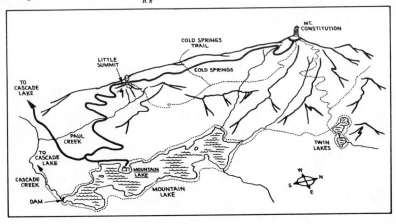

2 CASCADE FALLS

MOUNTAIN LAKE TO CASCADE LAKE
Hike along Cascade Creek past Rustic and Cascade Waterfalls to Cascade Lake. 2.7 miles.

Take the Cascade Lake trail south out of Mountain Lake Campground, continuing down stream beyond the dam. Watch for sections of old wooden flume used in the original water system near the trail.

Waterfalls in the last half of the trail. Watch for signs. When the trail crosses the highway, head up the road to the right to find trail on the other side.

Last stretch follows an aluminum flume built to stabilize the level of Cascade Lake. To avoid a useless climb over a ridge in back of the South End Campground, watch for view of the lake down a draw below the flume sections, picking up a way-trail down an old road to camp.

CASCADE FALLS
A wispy 100-foot skein of water in a cool green canyon. ¼ mile by trail.

Watch for sign off the main park road about 1 mile beyond the recreation center. Trail drops gradually to a marked overlook.

For a much smaller waterfall, take a trail up-river to the left. Rustic Falls in less than ¼ mile.

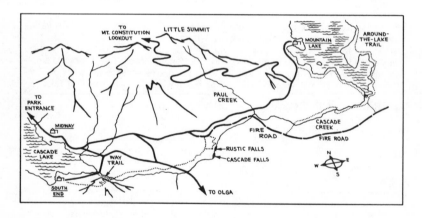

Cascade Falls

Picnic grounds at Cascade Lake

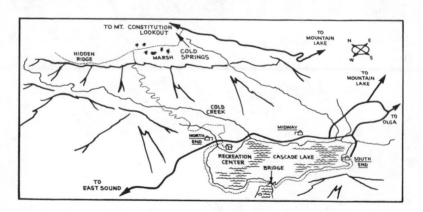

3   CASCADE LAKE

SOUTH END TRAIL

An easy, pleasant walk along Cascade Lake from the South End Campground to the recreation center with a wooden bridge, flowers, and modest views along the way.

Find the trail at the far end of the South End Campground near the lake shore. Leaving the camp, it wends across a rocky slope above the lake, dropping through an alder grove to a bridge across the inlet to the smaller, southern section of the lake. Keep to the right on trails that climb along a rocky bluff. Sedum and tiger lilies in season.

At the upper end of the lake the trail drops across a muddy area near the shore, crossing in front of the park ranger's house to the picnic and recreation center.

COLD SPRING TRAIL

Another drive-up and walk-back trail. This one from Cold Springs picnic area down a series of switchbacks with occasional views to the recreation center at Cascade Lake.

Take the trail out of Cold Springs picnic area through a wet but open creek bottom, turning downhill in about .3 mile at junction with a trail that leads around the mountain to Twin Lakes and the Mount Constitution tower.

About 2 miles to the lake.

Trillium

Campbell Lake and Skagit Bay from Mount Erie

B DECEPTION PASS STATE PARK

Salt water, fresh water, forests, and beaches—all overshadowed by a rushing tidal river beneath a spectacular bridge.

On both sides of Deception Pass between Fidalgo and Whidbey Islands, 18 miles from Mount Vernon. Or take the ferry from Mukilteo and drive up Whidbey Island from the south.

One of the most popular parks in the state. Over 2 million visitors a year. And no wonder! Two freshwater lakes, forest trails to beaches and scenic overlooks, tide pools full of sea life, a marsh with a wildlife of its own, and the tidal river that changes directions about every 6 hours.

The park is busy most summer weekends and packed on holidays. Some parts of it are open all year round.

Supervised swimming, playground facilities, and tide pool displays add to the attraction. And no motors are allowed on the lakes. Ideal for canoes.

MOUNT ERIE

See the Cascades from Garibaldi in Canada past Baker to Rainier with the San Juans, the island within an island in Campbell Lake, the deep blue hues of Puget Sound, and the Olympics.

About 8.6 miles from Deception Pass State Park but a "must" if you visit the area. Views from 1300 feet.

From the park, drive north about 4 miles beyond Pass Lake, taking a paved road sharply east on the north side of Campbell Lake. Watch for sign. Road turns north again just east of Lake Erie. A gravel spur leads east to the vista point. Watch for signs again. Summit about 4.6 miles from the Campbell Lake junction.

Park near buildings and walk to formal vista point. No camping. No water. Mountain climbers often practice on slopes south of summit.

CAMPGROUNDS

Bowman Bay—24 sites on Bowman Bay north of the pass. A wooded area overlooking the bay. The campground is often crowded and heavily used by trailers. All too little separation between units. Playground equipment. Restrooms. Piped water. State fee. Open summer only.

Cranberry Lake—Picnic sites in an open park-like area on the east end of Cranberry Lake. Playground. Dock. Boat rental concession. Restroom. Piped water. State fee.

Forest Camp—230 sites. No special trailer sites. On wooded loops in pleasant forest area north of Cranberry Lake. All sites except those at the older east end are well separated. Sites at west end are closest to the beach and lake. Restrooms. Piped water. State fee. Some sites open all year.

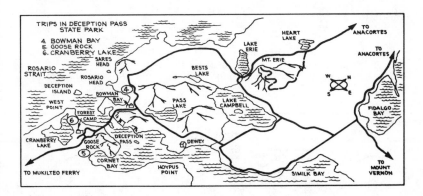

4 BOWMAN BAY

ROSARIO TRAIL

Hike along a bluff above Bowman Bay to sweeping views from Rosario Head.

Find trail at the east end of Bowman Bay Campground. Trail winds along the side of the steep bank above the bay ending near the boat dock on the west side of Rosario Head.

Climb onto grass alpine-like meadows above Rosario Bay for best views in all directions—from the bridge to the San Juans. 🚶

SEA LIFE

Tide pools and clams.

For best natural pools and low tide, drive to the Rosario Bay Picnic Area on the north side of the bridge. Divers prowl the rock pools around Rosario Head. Starfish and sea urchins at the lowest tides.

For clams—fewer and fewer each year—drive to Hoypus Point beyond the Cornet Bay boat-launching area. Park land extends south and west of the point. Butter clams on minus tides. 🚶

LIGHTHOUSE POINT

Camus flowers in May against green slopes and the dark blue of the sound on a trail that leads across a series of open bluffs to an unmanned Coast Guard light, a series of rock coves, and high views of Bowman Bay.

Follow the trail along the bay south of the fish hatchery, taking a fork to the right (west) beyond the first headland. Or walk around the headland at low tide to a flat spit of land.

Trail continues west along the pass with small sand coves, rest spots, and viewpoints sprinkled along the way. Clamber down a steep bank and up a ladder to inspect the automatic light in the point at the far end. Can be dangerous.

To return, follow way-trails along the north side of the peninsula. Spurs lead out on headland rocks. Look for a small arch carved by tidal action in one.

Best views of Bowman Bay and the campground from the highest point on the peninsula in the northeast corner. 🚶

CANOE PASS

Look up at the high Deception Pass Bridge from a small cove almost beneath the structure.

Take the trail along the east shore of the bay, south of the fish hatchery, continuing straight ahead at a fork just over the first headland. Trail climbs to an overlook point to the west before rounding a point and dropping down to the cove. 🚶

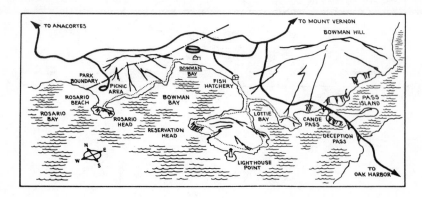

Tidal pool

Deception Pass and Cranberry Lake

5   GOOSE ROCK

Look down on most of the park. Cornet and Skagit Bays, east to the Cascades and west to the Olympics from flower-covered rocky slopes east of the bridge.

Find the trail at the south end of the bridge, heading east. Trail leaves either side of the highway. Follow the broad trail above the pass, taking almost any spur trail uphill, following unmarked paths to the highest point.

To return, follow the ridge crest east, taking a broad trail downhill.

Continue on the trail near the water and walk all the way around to Cornet Bay and around the park's group camp. Occasional spur trails lead down to rocky ledges close to the water.

PASS ISLAND

Paths lead from small parking area on the east side of the road to an historic marker and open grass meadows.

A plaque erected by the Daughters of the American Revolution tells how Vancouver discovered Deception Pass on June 10, 1792, thinking at first he had found a river.

Paths lead down the slopes of the island to pleasant resting places above the swift water of the pass.

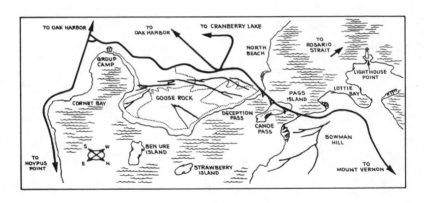

6   CRANBERRY LAKE

Marshes and beaver houses in addition to swimming and fishing.

Canoe into the marshy area on the south side of the lake to search for beaver houses hidden in the high weeds. Beaver, muskrat, and mink inhabit the marsh.

A paved ¼-mile loop trail leads south from the bathhouse at West Beach through a small dune area to a swamp and lake-viewing platform. Picnic tables en route.

Or hike into the bogs from the south end of the Cranberry Lake picnic area. No trails. Hop from log to log and bog to bog into a swamp world of frogs, lily pads, pollywogs, red wing blackbirds, canaries, purple honeysuckle, skunk cabbage, and bugs. A short walk leads into an entirely new ecological world. Beaver houses, however, cannot be reached on foot.

CRANBERRY LAKE TRAIL

From the Cranberry Lake picnic area across a soggy corner of the lake to Forest Campground.

A spur trail leads from the picnic area, north of the picnic area, around the lake, to the main road and the campground. Just far enough from the campgrounds and road to forget—for an instant, at least—that they are there.

BEACH WALKS

From the bridge to West Point and from West Point south along sand and gravel beaches looking out on the pass and Puget Sound.

From the bridge westward along the south side of the pass either walk along the beach—at low tide—or along a shore trail. Find the shore trail off the west end of the picnic road loop below the bridge. Pick your own way along the beach.

From West Point south follow the beach to the park boundary. 1 mile. Continue further at low tide, remembering that the beach is private property.

No clams on either beach. Agates are sometimes found on both with best picking on the west beach whenever the gravel is exposed by action of the waves.

Grass widow, a reddish-purple flower growing on Pass Island

Deception Pass Bridge from Pass Island

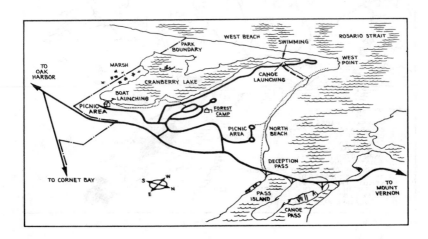

C   THE WEST SLOPE

Catalog all of the great things about Washington State and you'll find them here—on the west slope of the north Cascades.

In the one long section between Snoqualmie Pass and the Canadian border, find almost everything you could order:

Around Mount Baker, high flower-meadow vistas of the grand volcano with all its protecting peaks.

Up the Skagit River and its tributaries, deep forests, eagles, hot springs and waterfalls.

On the loop highway between the drainages of the Stillaguamish, all of that with rushing rivers too.

And, finally, in off-highway crannies of Snoqualmie and Stevens passes, lookouts, still more waterfalls and scenic vista points.

Highway I-5 leads to all of the gateway roads out of Bellingham, Mount Vernon, Arlington, Everett and Seattle. Paved state roads lead up the major valleys with Forest Service logging roads taking the visitor to the most choice recreation points.

And you can travel here by foot or car. Follow spring up into the mountains and follow autumn all the way back down with the exact time of each season subject to the whims of weather, year to year.

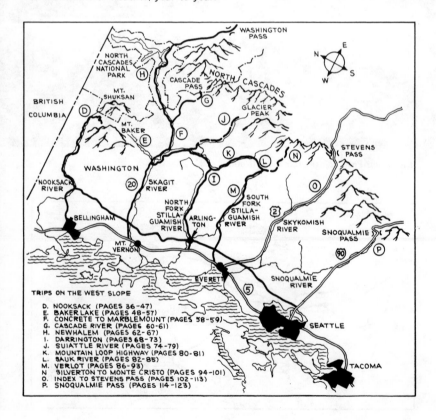

TRIPS ON THE WEST SLOPE

Footbridge over the Suiattle River

Picture Lake and Mount Shukshan

D NOOKSACK RIVER

From shaded river trails to blazing mountain views. Mount Baker and Mount Shuksan dominate the valley. But leaf-imprint rocks, waterfalls, big trees, alpine flower meadows, and teeming salmon runs give it greater dimension.

From the freeway through Bellingham (watch for the Mount Baker exit sign No. 255), drive east on Highway 542. The pavement ends at Mount Baker Lodge. A gravel road continues to Austin Pass and Kulshan Ridge.

Glacier Creek Road

Mount Baker often hides some of its better views around corners or over ridges. But not so on Glacier Creek road. Here the mountain booms out a full view with no obstructions at all.

Drive about ½ mile east from the Glacier Ranger Station on Highway 542, turning south on Glacier Creek road No. 3904 for another 8 miles. The road climbs steadily over easy switchbacks with views much of the way. Just beyond the Kulshan Cabin trail parking area (7½ miles) the road ducks into timber and then leaps out on the edge of the mountain again, up a single, steep pitch, to a turnaround viewpoint (4000).

The view spreads north down the Glacier Creek valley and eastward to Baker, taking in Roosevelt and Coleman Glaciers, Black Buttes (Colfax, Lincoln, and Seward Peaks). Pretty even on a misty day. Good sunsets too. Huckleberries along the upper sections of the road. ➛

THOMPSON CREEK SALMON RUN

Thompson Creek receives the biggest run of spawning salmon on the Nooksack River system. At its peak, the lower mile of the small stream literally boils with struggling fish. However, the salmon only run heavily every other year. Odd-numbered years offer the biggest displays. Best time is in late August and September.

The easiest viewpoint is from the Thompson Creek bridge. From Highway 542, drive south on the Thompson Creek road about a mile. The run can also be observed in Gallop Creek in the town of Glacier. But the run there nowhere equals the Thompson Creek show. ➛

CAMPGROUNDS

Douglas Fir—2 miles east of Glacier. 30 sites, some near the river, others on a shaded forest loop. Piped water. Pit toilets. Community kitchen. Fee camp. Closed during week.

Nooksack—4 miles from Glacier. 19 units, most away from the river in heavy undergrowth. Piped water. Pit toilets. Fee camp.

Excelsior—7 miles from Glacier. 12 units spread out over an open-timbered gravel bar but set back from the river. Access road steep and narrow. Water from creek near entrance. Pit toilets. Closed during week.

Silver Fir—13 miles from Glacier. 19 tent and 12 trailer units with most sites on the river. Others back on forest loops. Sandbar at upper end of campground provides wading for children. Piped water. Kitchen. Pit toilets. Fee camp.

Hannegan—6 sites in a primitive camp in an open brushy alpine area at the end of the Hannegan road, about 5 miles from the paved highway. Used largely by hikers and packers heading into the North Cascades. Shelter. Pit toilets.

Bridge—6 sites in a forest area on the Nooksack River. Drive east of the Glacier Ranger station, turning south on Glacier Creek road and then east on Deadhorse road No. 3907. Campground in about 4½ miles, just west of the closed old bridge.

Canyon—6 sites off Canyon Creek road. Turn north on Canyon Creek road just east of Douglas Fir Campground. Camp in little more than 6 miles.

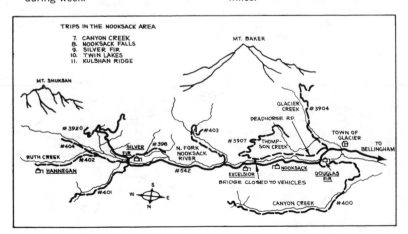

TRIPS IN THE NOOKSACK AREA
7. CANYON CREEK
8. NOOKSACK FALLS
9. SILVER FIR
10. TWIN LAKES
11. KULSHAN RIDGE

7   CANYON CREEK

HORSESHOE BEND TRAIL

A very pleasant 2-mile stroll along an interpretive trail to absolutely no place at all. The trail leaves the highway-end of the Douglas Fir Campground beneath the concrete bridge (or from the highway at the southeast corner of the bridge). It wanders along the Nooksack through lush, river-bottom vine maple, past an old log seat carved out of a stump over a bridge and up a stairway.

The first part ends next to a noisy river rapids. The trail then climbs quickly to a ledge and stays above the river until it ends at water level again.

The trail does exactly what it's designed to do: Provide a relaxing end to a busy day. Time? Just as long as you want to spend. 🏃

EXCELSIOR RIDGE TRAIL

A hike of less than 2 miles leads past two pretty tarn-like lakes to meadow glimpses of Mount Baker, Church and Bearpaw Mountains and the length of the heavily logged Canyon Creek basin.

Follow the Canyon Creek road No. 400 for 12½ miles, taking a fork to the left at that point. Find a parking area and trail sign in a mile. The trail climbs to the two Damfino Lakes (4500) in about a mile. A great place to camp, picnic or prowl.

Walk another mile to the first of many high meadows with views. Reach the top of Excelsior mountain in still another mile—a total of 3 miles from the road.

LEAF-IMPRINT ROCKS

Imprints of leaves and fossilized plants, millions of years old, in uplifted rock deposits right beside the road.

To find two fossil sites, take the first logging road north beyond the Douglas Fir Campground—Canyon Creek road No. 400.

For the first location, drive just short of the 4-mile marker post on the right—and just beyond as well—watching for layered, vertical formations in the road cuts to the right.

For the second (2.5 miles from highway) turn right on spur road No. 4007. Find imprints in a cliff about 300 feet before the road junctions with No. 4007A.

Black, crumbly rock contains matted fossils of stems and stalks. Flat sandstone sections often bear imprints of leaves. No need to dig out new rock in the first location. Seek samples in broken material on the lower side of the road. Imprints of complete palm-like leaves have been found in that area.

For sea shell fossils turn north up the road marked Church Mountain Trail ¾ mile beyond the Nooksack Campground. Drive to the first creek crossing where the stream goes over the road, 1¾ miles from highway. 🚗

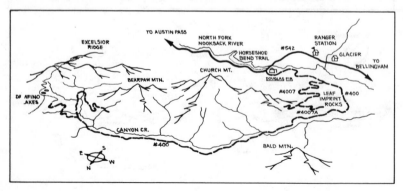

Leaf fossils found in rock along road No. 4007

8   NOOKSACK FALLS

One of the largest-volume waterfalls in the forests of northwestern Washington. The full Nooksack River plunges 170 feet into a tight gorge with a thundering, earth-shaking roar.

Watch for a sign indicating the falls about 7 miles from the Glacier Ranger Station on Highway 542. Drive ½ mile on forest road No. 403 to the bridge. The falls are on the right.

A steel fence rims the steep cliffs around the falls, but still approach the edge with caution. Full views of the torrent come in peeks and glimpses between clefts in the rock along the high trail downstream. The falls are on property owned by Puget Sound Power and Light Co. Observe warnings. Can be dangerous. ⋏

SKYLINE DIVIDE TRAIL

A hike of about 2 miles brings tremendous views of Mount Baker, Mt. Shuksan and Excelsior Ridge from the high alpine meadows of the Skyline Divide (5800).

Drive about ½ mile east from the Glacier Ranger Station turning south on the Glacier Creek road No. 3904. Then, in about 300 feet, turn east on Deadhorse road No. 3907. Follow the logging road 14 miles as it makes its way first east and then back to the west, climbing in a series of switchbacks over the river valley with views toward the ridge, Church and Bearpaw Mountains. Trail sign and parking area on the right side of the road.

Trail, on the left, climbs sharply 2 miles (first views within a mile) before breaking out into alpine meadows, continuing on south 3 miles more along the ridge with no particular ending. Big, long views of Baker most of the way. ⋏

BIG FIR AREA

A 4-mile stretch of forest beginning about 10 miles east of the Glacier Ranger Station containing prime examples of original-growth Douglas fir, hemlock, and cedar and the natural forest undergrowth common to such stands.

The trees are in the North Fork Nooksack Natural Area—a formal preserve, a mile deep along the north side of the highway, which will be kept in its natural state.

There are no trails or markings describing the nature of the plant life in the preserve. Each hiker must pick his own way through the area and seek his own means of identifying the natural features. ⋏

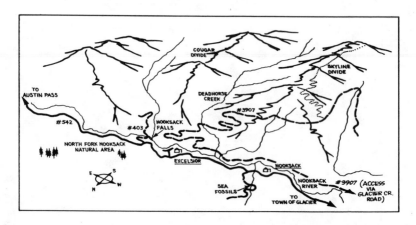

Mount Baker from Skyline Ridge. Black Buttes on right skyline

9   SILVER FIR

Three logging roads lead to easy and grand views of Mount Shuksan from the Silver Fir Campground.

For the quickest view, drive east on the Hannegan road No. 402 less than ¼ mile, turning off the paved highway just before reaching the bridge at the Silver Fir Campground. For even fuller views, continue on road No. 402 less than 2 miles taking the first spur road to the right. Continuous views of the mountain clear to the end of the spur, about 3 miles.

For the third viewpoint, drive up the main highway toward Mount Baker Lodge and Heather Meadows, taking road No. 3920 spur to the left on a sharp switchback about 5 miles from the Silver Fir Campground. Drive less than 1 mile until road rounds a razor-like ridge. Views of the mountain looking up White Salmon Creek. The vertical end of Hanging Glacier is about 700 feet high.

RUTH MOUNTAIN VIEW

An easy 2-mile hike in late summer leads to flower meadows and views of snow-topped Ruth Mountain (7105). The trail leaves Hannegan Camp at the end of the Hannegan road No. 402, about 5 miles from the main highway at Shuksan.

Ruth Mountain comes into view within the first mile. Brush gives way to meadows in less than 2 miles. Views too of Mount Sefrit, Nooksack Ridge, and Granite Mountain. Trail eventually leads to Hannegan Pass, 4 miles.

BEAVER DAMS

With extreme care, lots of patience, and an immense amount of good luck, almost any visitor can watch the busy beaver work along Anderson Creek. But even if the beaver fails to show, his handiwork will be everywhere apparent.

At the entrance to the Silver Fir Campground take the logging road to the left instead of the campground road. Follow the road (Anderson Creek road No. 398) about 2 miles, watching out over the swampy flats to the right for signs of dams and beaver. Best examples are most likely near Barometer Creek where the road splits at a Y, 1½ miles from highway.

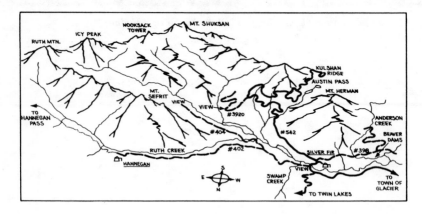

Nooksack Ridge from Ruth Creek Trail

10   TWIN LAKES

A spectacular alpine camping area. Two crystal lakes at 5200 feet tucked into flower and heather meadows and surrounded by mountains.

But not an area to plan on. This county road, maintained by miners, is seldom open before mid-July and some years not at all. The last mile of the steep, narrow, very rough road is always difficult and occasionally impassable. And some years the road may be open while the lake basin is still packed with snow. If firm trip plans are required, check with the ranger in advance. And leave town prepared to backpack your gear at least the last 2 miles.

Camp at developed sites between the two lakes and on a bench above the lower lake. There are a few sites on the north side of the upper lake for those equipped to pack their equipment. Campers and hikers should treat the area with loving care. Its beauty is particularly fragile. Thoughtless visitors can add nothing, but destroy much.

Drive 13½ miles east of the Glacier Ranger Station, turning north on road No. 401 just beyond the highway maintenance barns at Shuksan. 7 miles to the lakes, or park at the creek crossing beyond the Tomyhoi Lake Trail and hike the rest of the way, 1½ miles. 🚶

GOLD PANNING

Gold panners sometimes try their luck in Swamp Creek, which originates in the gold mine areas of Twin Lakes. Pan where the creek crosses the Hannegan road about ½ mile from the highway or along the upper reaches of road No. 401 to Twin Lakes. No gold is guaranteed.

GOLD RUN PASS

A 2-mile walk leads to views north of peaks near the Canadian border and south of overpowering Mount Baker.

Take the Tomyhoi Lake Trail off the road toward Twin Lakes (see above) 4½ miles from the main highway. The trail climbs alternately through meadows and forest to the top of the pass. Drop downhill another 2 miles to Tomyhoi Lake or explore ridges at the pass. 🚶

GARGETT MINE TRAIL

When the snow is gone, a pleasant walk of a mile or more over open alpine flower slopes. Some years the trail is blocked all summer by snowfields, tricky to cross even with an ice ax.

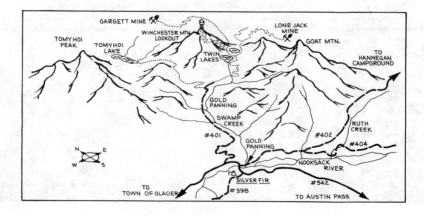

Twin Lakes and Mount Baker

Trail starts north between the lakes. At ¼ mile, keep right at the junction with the trail to Winchester Mountain Lookout.

The mine trail, little used but still easy to follow, skirts the northeast side of Winchester Mountain climbing toward Low Pass and then along the ridge crest to High Pass. Views of Canadian peaks, Mount Larrabee, the Pleiades, and Skagit Ridge. Trail eventually winds to Gargett Mine, 3 miles, on the slopes of Larrabee.

To reach the Winchester Mountain Lookout—1½ miles—turn uphill at the junction. Again, the trail may be blocked, some years, by dangerous patches of snow. Trail switchbacks to a lookout atop the peak which is operated on an emergency basis only.

LONE JACK MINE TRAIL

A steep 1-mile trail to a private gold-mining area.

Take trail through the saddle at the east end of the upper lake. At about ¼ mile, turn off on a spur trail to the right. The trail hangs on the side of the mountain for about another ½ mile then drops VERY steeply to the mine. A few tumbling buildings, debris, and one plugged mine shaft.

11   KULSHAN RIDGE

Heaven knows how many visitors mistake the most obvious and spectacular peak in the Heather Meadows-Mount Baker Lodge area for Mount Baker. The big, rugged mountain, of course, is Shuksan, one of the most photographed in the U.S. And Baker, as usual, is hidden, reserving its views for those willing to drive a little bit farther or hike a little bit higher.

Artist Point parking lot on Kulshan Ridge about 2 miles beyond the lodge at the end of the highway, offers the easiest views of the evasive Mount Baker. But the sometimes-road, as often walked as driven, is seldom clear of snow before the end of July and many years not until late August—if at all. So be sure to leave town prepared to walk at least part of the way in snow.

Drive as far as the road permits and then walk on to the parking area just beyond Austin Pass at 4700 feet. Views of Baker, Shuksan, and Ptarmigan Ridge—all rising above snow-patched alpine flower meadows. ▰

ARTIST POINT

A favorite spot for photographers seeking pictures of Mount Baker at her best. No formal trails. No signs. But an easy ½-mile walk along tourist paths to a series of viewpoints atop a ridge.

From the parking area, walk out the ridge extending off to the southeast. Along with Baker, more views of Shuksan, and the lesser ridges southeast above Baker Lake. Find a reflecting pool on the south side of the point. Either walk over the top and drop about 100 feet down or contour around the east side. For best pictures of Baker, get there before noon. 👫

COLEMAN PINNACLE VIEW

A level 1-mile scenic walk with continuous views of Mount Baker plus occasional down-valley glimpses of Baker Lake. Take the Chain Lake trail from the west end of the Artist Point parking area to the pass-like alpine area at the far end of Table Mountain, stopping before the trail turns and drops down toward Chain Lakes.

Watch for marmots in the rocks both above and below the trail and for the modest magenta paintbrush among the more colorful alpine flowers alongside the trail.

Chain Lake: Another mile, mostly downhill. 👫

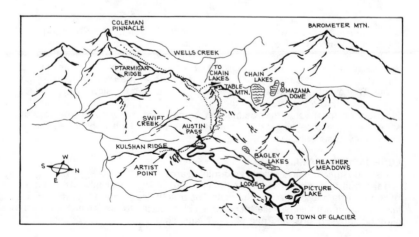

Ptarmigan Ridge

PTARMIGAN RIDGE

Add another mile or more to the easy walk (above) and pick up still more vistas of high meadows, deep valleys and Mount Baker.

From the saddle where the Chain Lake trail turns right (east) continue forward toward the mountain on a path that drops downhill slightly and then climbs again to Ptarmigan Ridge.

Snow sometimes covers the ridge all year. But the pathway, at least to the first ridge, is generally clear (observe it from the saddle). The trail continues on to Camp Kiser, an unmarked alpine area. ⚑

TABLE MOUNTAIN

A steep and, in spots, precipitous, ½-mile climb from the Artist Point parking area on Kulshan Ridge to the top of Table Mountain for unencumbered views of all surrounding peaks.

Take the Chain Lake trail out of the far end of the parking lot, watching for an uphill trail in about ¼ mile. Trail switchbacks very steeply to the plateau-top of the mountain. Definitely not for the queasy or those new to the ways of mountain trails.

At the top, the trail crosses a pretty alpine meadow dotted with cold pools to a steep snowfield, extremely dangerous to cross without proper mountaineering gear and training. ⚑

Mount Baker from road No. 385

E   BAKER LAKE

A busy recreation area that seems to get busier every year.

The man-made lake is the biggest attraction. But the mountains on both sides offer a wide variety of view drives and hikes, hot springs, waterfalls, alpine scenes and forest lookouts.

Take I-5 north to Mt. Vernon, turning east on the North Cascades Highway (Exit No. 230). About 4 miles beyond the Hamilton-Lyman exit, take the Baker Lake-Grandy Lake road to the north. Mount Baker National Forest boundary in about 12 miles.

CAMPGROUNDS

Horseshoe Cove—27 units in second-growth timber, long, sloping swimming area behind a log boom ideal for children. No lifeguard. Piped water. Flush toilets. Charge camp.

Bayview—Organized group camp. Reservations only.

Boulder Creek—10 units in wooded site along a glacial creek. Many who plan trips into mountain areas prefer it to the busy lakeshore camps. Pit toilets.

Baker Lake—16 units on an open, unshaded peninsula. All sites are near the water. But little beach. Boat launching. Views of Blum, Shuksan, and Baker from shore. Pit toilets. Charge camp.

Park Creek—12 units on Park Creek off Morovitz Creek road No. 3816. About half the sites along the creek. All in pleasant, shaded forest area. Gets heavy use despite the fact it's away from the lake. Pit toilets.

Morovitz Creek—3 units, almost always occupied. Secluded camp spots off the Morovitz road No. 3816 in a shaded, big-timber area near a small, pretty stream and pond. Pit toilet.

Shannon Creek—20 units in wooded area near lake. Most sites on wooded loops away from the lake. Pit toilets.

Maple Grove—6 units on the east side of the lake about 1½ miles northeast of Horseshoe Cove. Boat and trail camp. Sites back a little from the lake with views of Mount Baker. Not busy, usually. Water from nearby streams. Pit toilets.

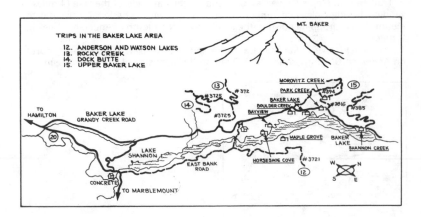

12   ANDERSON AND WATSON LAKES

Two clusters of high, alpine lakes in spectacular meadow country less than 3 miles from the end of a high and scenic but poorly maintained logging road.

Trail starts uphill sharply from a parking area and then climbs briskly up and down to the lakes trail junction in a short 2 miles. Trail uphill to the left climbs steeply over a ridge and then down to the two big Watson lakes (4475 feet). Views over both from a steep meadow before you reach the lakes.

Trail to the right leads to the first of several smaller but more open Anderson Lakes in less than a half-mile. Bear off to the right at the first lake for a breathtaking view of Mount Baker from a pretty meadow just across the creek. Other views, from both lakes, of Mount Watson and Bacon Peak.

(For a vigorous side trip, climb to Anderson Butte (5420), site of an old lookout. Watch for trail to the left before you reach the main junction in maybe 1 ¾ miles.)

Camping at Watson lakes on the first lake or on open meadows between the lakes. Camping in the Anderson Lake area on meadows everywhere. Spend a day at either lake area or a weekend at both.

Drive across the Upper Baker Dam about 1 ¼ miles south of Horseshoe Cove Campground, bearing north (left) on Anderson Creek road No. 3721. About 10 ½ miles to the trailhead. 🚶 🚐

SHADOW OF THE SENTINELS

A ½-mile nature loop-trail through old-growth timber, some more than 500 years old. Prime examples of towering Douglas fir, silver fir, and hemlock are identified along the trail together with other forest plants common to the region.

Drive ½ mile north of the Koma Kulshan Guard Station, 11 ½ miles north of Concrete. Watch for parking area and sign on the right side of the road. 🚶

EAST BANK TRAIL

Stroll from a dusty road through cool forest to a pleasant bay on Baker Lake.

Trail ends at Maple Grove Campground on the east side of the lake (4 miles), winding through pleasant timber above the lake with occasional views out at Mount Baker, dropping down to the small bay at the mouth of Anderson Creek in 2 miles.

Drive over Upper Baker Lake Dam (see Anderson-Watson Lakes) bearing north on Anderson Creek road No. 3721. Trail on the west side of the road in 1 mile. 🚶

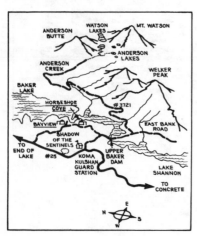

Watson Lake

Mount Shuksan from Dillard Point

13   ROCKY CREEK

DILLARD POINT LOOKOUT

By far the easiest view in the Baker Lake area. Drive directly to the lookout tower at 2400 feet. Parking area, picnic tables, pit toilets near the tower.

Follow road No. 3725 up Rocky Creek 3.5 miles bearing right at the junction. In another .7 mile turn right at the Dillard Point Lookout sign onto road No. 372B. The lookout in .7 mile. Views of Mount Baker, Shuksan, the Pickets, Blum, Hagan, Bacon, with glimpses of White Horse—all above Baker and Shannon Lakes. Huckleberries, too, in the fall.

SCHRIEBERS MEADOWS

An easy walk through open-timbered huckleberry and flower meadows about as long as you want to make it.

A damp area, infested with mosquitos through much of the summer. But bugless in the fall when the meadows turn rich with berries and color.

Trail at the end of road No. 372—5.2 miles beyond the Loomis Nooksack-Sulphur Creek road junction and 8.7 miles from the highway at Rocky Creek bridge. Look for a trail sign about 25 yards off the road on a parking spur to the left.

Cross the trail bridge over Sulphur Creek and then walk through increasingly open timber, past occasional small ponds with reflected glimpses of Mount Baker to the north.

In 1 mile the trail crosses three tumbling streams from Easton Glacier on the south side of Mount Baker.

Hike on another mile—the trail switchbacks steeply now through forest—to the lower Morovitz Meadow, with more views. Trail continues on either to Park Butte at 5450 feet or to Baker Pass, both in a total of 4 miles.

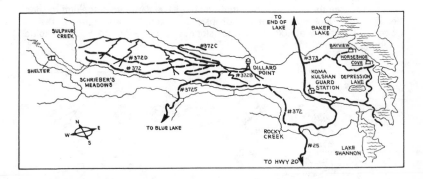

14   DOCK BUTTE

A scenic drive and scenic hike lead to a high ridge overlooking Baker Lake with still more scenic views of all the major peaks in the Mount Baker area.

Take the Rocky Creek road No. 3725 west at the Rocky Creek bridge less than a half-mile inside the Mount Baker National Forest boundary about 10 miles north of Concrete. After 7 miles turn left onto road No. 3770, following the signs to Blue Lake and Dock Butte trails, another 4 miles. Good views of Baker, Shuksan, Blum, and other North Cascade peaks along the last 3 miles.

At the end of the road, trail to the Butte and Blue Lake (see below) climbs out of a clear-cut to a trail junction over a slight ridge. Dock Butte trail, to the right, climbs steadily up a series of switchbacks with increasing views out toward Baker and Shuksan. In less than 1 mile, an open meadow—flowers in summer, colors in fall—atop a beautiful alpine ridge. Views swing from the Twin Sisters to the east around through Baker and Shuksan, up the Baker River valley to the Pickets, and westward to Blum, Hagan, and Bacon.

Follow the ridge trail south past pleasant pools, grey outcrops of rock, grown-over mine prospects, weathered trees, and camping spots.

The trail, however, becomes increasingly difficult to follow the farther south it goes, disappearing completely in some places. Trails bearing to the left afford access to a cross-ridge with views of Glacier Peak, White Horse, and White Chuck.

Bear to the right along the rising ridge to the south to find Dock Butte in another mile. A very steep trail shoots up the west side of the pointed butte to a former lookout site where Mount Rainier is added to the vista. Probably not for novices or the queasy. ⚑

BLUE LAKE

Named precisely. A pretty, clear-blue lake tucked into the base of the Dock Butte ridge. A pleasant, easy trip. 1 mile.

Take the trail to the left at the junction about 100 yards from the end of road No. 3770 (see Dock Butte). The trail drops down through a timber area to the attractive 13-acre lake at 4000 feet. Talus slopes rise at the far end. But sub-alpine meadows surround the rest. ⚑

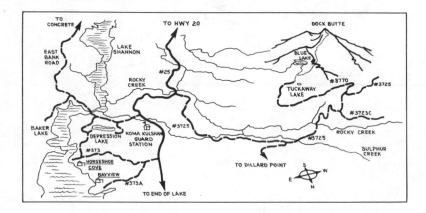

Mount Baker from Dock Butte

15   UPPER BAKER LAKE

BAKER HOT SPRINGS
A great and often crowded place (18,000 visitors a year) to soak tired feet and bathe—if you care and dare to. Less than ¼ mile off the road by very easy trail to a 110-degree mineral spring bubbling into a man-made wooden tub. Changing house, outhouse and picnic tables too.

Take road No. 3816 off the main lake highway from the lake at the Tarrs Resort-Park Creek Campground junction. In 3.3 miles watch for parking area and trail signs on left, on uphill side of the road. Very popular. Nude swimming banned between 9 a.m. and 7 p.m.

RAINBOW FALLS
The biggest waterfall in the Baker Lake area. Rainbow Creek plunges 200 feet into a steep canyon.

Drive 4.3 miles from the lake highway on road No. 3816 (see above), past the hot springs parking area, taking a sharp right turn at a junction in ½ mile. Falls—a solid rainbow if the sun is right—on the right in another half mile off road No. 385. Watch for sign.

Trail leads to a viewpoint in 15 yards. Use caution in going beyond established areas. Slick rock and cliffs make a close approach to the falls hazardous. The ground slopes gently near the road but drops off sharply nearer the stream. There is no view at the bottom of the drop-off.

BAKER RIVER TRAIL
Peace here in the twin pleasures of towering trees and a busy river. Stroll 1 mile or 3 in the solitude of a virgin forest broken only by the occasional surprise glimpses of the surrounding peaks—Mount Blum (view in ½ mile) Easy Ridge (in 2 miles) and Whatcom Peak (just a little further).

Drive beyond the end of Baker Lake on the main forest road No. 25, turning north (left) at the four-way junction (watch for Griners Shelter sign), driving another half-mile to a shelter cabin and the start of the trail. Trail leads into North Cascades National Park in about 1½ miles.

MOUNT BAKER VIEWS
Mount Baker, difficult to see from highways near the lake, comes out of hiding completely on the Shuksan Creek road No. 394. Turn north off the lake highway

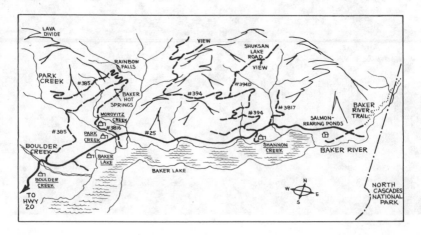

Baker Hot Springs

near the upper end of Baker Lake, about 3 miles beyond Baker Lake Resort. Either follow No. 394 to the end with views of Mount Baker most of the way, or take the Shuksan Lake road spur to the right for vistas of Mount Baker, Baker Lake, and Mount Blum. (The spur does not go to Shuksan Lake, however.) Poor views of Shuksan from either spur. Too close to the mountain.

SALMON-REARING PONDS

Large, man-made gravel beds at the upper end of Baker Lake provide a near-natural setting in which salmon spawn. Brood sockeye are trapped in pens below Baker Dam and trucked to the ponds in tanks. The spawn hatches naturally in the gravel beds and the young fish are eventually released downstream. Spawning fish can be seen generally in late September and October.

Drive beyond the end of Baker Lake on the main forest road No. 25. At the four-way junction beyond the lake, turn south. Main ponds are fenced but are often open to the public. Salmon can also be seen during the peak of the fall run in the unfenced, pond-like sections of Intake Creek at the end of short unmarked spur trails to the right (west) of the road to the main hatchery complex.

F   CONCRETE TO MARBLEMOUNT

FISH ELEVATOR

Spawning salmon, trying to reach the upper Baker River, swim into tank traps below Baker Dam and are trucked to rearing ponds above the lake.

In Concrete, cross the bridge just east of town and turn sharply right into a parking area below the bridge and near steel structures over the river. Tourist ramps lead out over trapping pens where salmon are caught in tanks that are lifted out of the river and emptied into trucks backed out on special ramps. Taped-message installation. Trucking operation takes place during the height of the fall salmon run.

EAGLE SANCTUARY

Hundreds of magnificent bald eagles winter here, feeding on dead salmon which have spawned in the Skagit River.

From December through February observe the birds—as many as 300 at a time—along both sides of the river between Rockport and Marblemount. Take your binoculars.

The birds are often most visible in the tops of trees. But if you're lucky you can see groups of them haggling over fish on sandbars or river banks. This is a Nature Conservancy sanctuary aimed at preserving an important wintering ground for these grand birds. Observe, but don't disturb!

SAUK MOUNTAIN

High views of the Skagit and Sauk valleys from a zigzag road to a ridge just below Sauk Mountain Lookout, another 2 miles by trail.

Turn north on the first road **west** of Rockport State Park on Highway 20. After about a mile the road starts a series of tedious switchbacks. Watch for a road to the right in about 7 miles from the highway to a new turnaround parking area at the trailhead.

Views all the way up with Mount Baker joining the vista at the top of the ridge.

Lookout trail switchbacks across very steep flower slopes to an unmanned lookout building with views of the valleys, Marblemount, Concrete, Glacier, Baker, Shuksan, White Horse, White Chuck, and Pugh.

The trail can be treacherous. Use care, avoid dislodging rocks and don't short-cut switchbacks. A very steep slope!

CAMPGROUNDS

Rockport State Park—50 trailer sites, 4 walk-in tent sites, 4 with walk-in shelters. Restrooms. Water. Nature trails. Vistas. On Highway 20 about 10 miles east of Concrete. State fee.

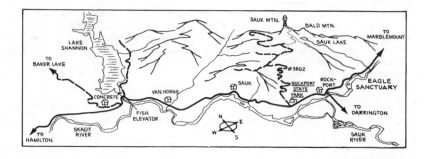

Bald eagles near Rockport

Family outing at Cascade Pass

G CASCADE RIVER

CASCADE PASS

The queen of all the short Cascade mountain hikes. Longer than most in this book—3 miles, but easy—the trail leads to a spectacular alpine pass with views in every direction, in North Cascades National Park.

Follow the Cascade River road 20 miles east from Marblemount to its end in a parking and picnic area. Views here of the hanging glaciers on Johannesberg Mountain to the south and of Cascade Pass to the east.

A trail switchbacks very gradually through timber topping out at last on a long traverse toward the pass across open, alpine meadows with long, constant views. Paintbrush, monkey flowers, penstemons, and whole hillsides of red columbine.

From the pass, hike north to the top of Sahale Arm for more spectacular views and higher heather meadows. This entire fragile high area is for day-use only. No camping at all. Pit toilets off the trail on both sides of the pass.

HIDDEN LAKE TRAIL

It's 4 miles to Hidden Lake lookout. But a 2-mile walk leads to heather-meadow views over open slopes below the higher ridges. Take your lunch and spend an hour here watching marmots and comparing the splendor of a small, high valley to the squalor of a city street.

Turn off the Cascade River road 2 miles east of Marble Creek Campground onto Sibley Creek road No. 3503. Road climbs to view of Snowking and Lookout Mountains. Trail, at end of road, climbs 1 mile through timber before breaking out on open slopes.

CAMPGROUNDS

Marble Creek—28 units, some along the Cascade River, others back on forest loops. Newer units nearest the highway. Others down narrow roads, difficult for trailers, at the far end of the camp. 9 miles from Marblemount. Pit toilets. Fee camp.

Mineral Park—22 units on both sides of the North Fork of the Cascade River, and along the main river. A few units oriented to the river but most in the big timber. 17 miles from Marblemount. Pit toilets.

Johannesburg—5 primitive sites near the parking area at the end of the Cascade River road. A walk-in hiker camp for those returning from or leaving for the park backcountry.

Note: All 'backcountry camping within the park by permit. Camping is limited to designated sites along trails. Wilderness camps allowed at least a mile off trails—by permit also.

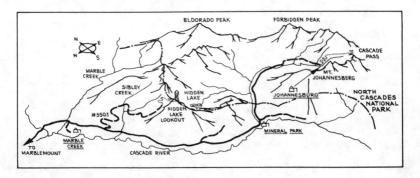

Diablo Lake and Davis Peak

H   NEWHALEM

Starting point of the formal Skagit Tours sponsored by Seattle City Light. Persons wanting to take the tours, however, must make reservations in advance through the tour office, City Light Building, Seattle.

A number of features can be visited informally:

Gorge Powerhouse—Park in town and walk across the bridge to the powerhouse at the upper end of the small community. The observation gallery is open most of the time to casual visitors. Four generators produce 175,000 kilowatts from water behind Gorge Dam.

Ladder Creek Falls—Just behind the power house take a marked trail for a ¼-mile loop walk around a series of waterfalls in a rock garden setting. Lighted at night.

Old Number Six—A steam engine designed to be climbed over. All that's left of the rolling stock of the old Seattle Skagit River Railway built in connection with dam construction. Just to the right of the highway at the upper end of the community.

THORNTON CREEK VIEWS

A rough road climbs steeply, hanging onto hillsides in places, to views of the Upper Skagit valley, Marblemount, Teebone Ridge, and the snows of Snowfield and Colonial Peaks.

Turn north on the Thornton Creek road No. 3745 2 miles south of Newhalem. At the end of the road in 5 miles walk down an abandoned spur another 2 miles for a bigger viewpoint.

NEWHALEM CREEK VIEWS

Big Devil Peak and Teebone Ridge stand out to the south and the Pickets rise in the north from Newhalem Creek road No. 376. Take the first road south between the Goodell Creek Campground and Newhalem, keeping uphill to the right within the first mile.

Road ends at the park boundary about 1 ½ miles from the highway. Walk up the road toward the Newhalem Creek backcountry camp for increasing views of the Pickets within the first mile, Big Devil and Teebone at the end of the trail.

CAMPGROUNDS

Goodell Creek—25 units and two group camps. In North Cascades National Park. Just south of Newhalem. Pit toilets. Water.

Bacon Creek—A 12-site picnic area 5 miles north of Marblemount. Well shaded, big timber and vine maple. Gravel bar on creek affords wading for children. Pit toilets.

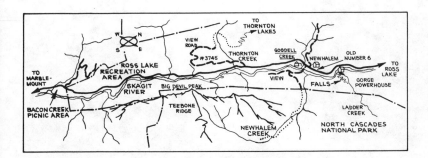

Diablo Lake and Pyramid Peak

16   DIABLO AND ROSS DAMS

THUNDER CREEK TRAIL

A pleasant stroll of about 1 mile (or more) along a level trail on the Thunder Arm of Diablo Lake. Find the trail near the water at the south end of Colonial Creek Campground. It follows the arm of Diablo Lake which gradually dwindles into Thunder Creek at a bridge, 1 mile. The trail continues on up Thunder Creek. Walk as far as you like.

ROSS DAM TRAIL

Hike to Ross Dam from the North Cascades Highway and trails leading up Ross Lake to Big Beaver Creek and down to Diablo Dam.

Drive east beyond Colonial Creek Campground 4 miles to a trailhead on the left side of the road. Trail switchbacks .8 mile down to the dam and a resort. An easy walk down but a short, stiff hike back up.

Cross the top of the dam to reach the Big Beaver trail. Take the spur road down to Diablo Lake to find the head of the trail (see below) that leads back to Diablo Dam.

DIABLO LAKE TRAIL

Ride a City Light work tug to the base of Ross Dam and then hike back 3 miles to Diablo Dam.

Catch the tug at the Diablo Dam powerhouse. Check the current schedule with Seattle City Light in Newhalem.

Find the trail from the head of the lake back to Diablo at the suspension bridge below Ross Dam. Trail climbs inland above the lake and ends in the Diablo Resort.

Drive about a mile beyond the bridge below the town of Diablo, taking the first road left. Drive across the top of Diablo dam to the tug dock.

For views of the dam itself, stop on the far side and walk down a path to the top of the incline railway, used to bring tour patrons to the lake from the Diablo town-site.

CAMPGROUND

Colonial Creek—165 sites on both sides of the North Cascades Highway on Thunder Arm of Diablo Lake, 23 miles northeast of Marblemount. 65 units north of the highway, 100 units south including a new 5-trailer loop. Boat launching. No units oriented to the lake. All on pleasant wooded loops. Some walk-in sites. Piped water. Restrooms. Charge camp.

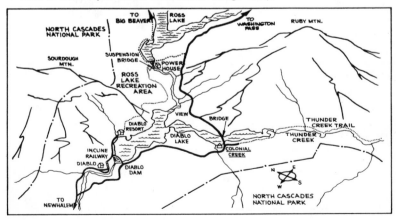

17   ROSS LAKE

Rent a boat on Ross Lake—or better yet, paddle your own canoe—and decide for yourself whether Seattle City Light should be permitted to raise Ross dam flooding out Big Beaver valley, one of the most primitive in the Northwest.

Boat to the Beaver Creek campground on the lake and then follow easy up-and-down trails around quiet marshes, beaver ponds and meadows and through groves of big trees,

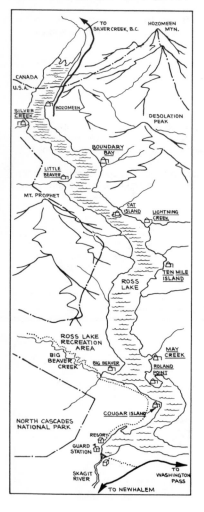

making mental note as you go that all that you see could be lost.

Make it a walk-and-write trip. After you've walked, write the Mayor of Seattle and any of the city's council members to let them know how you feel. Agencies—city, state and federal—immediately involved in the issue change from time to time as the dispute over raising the dam moves through the political mill. But local officials always play a key role.

And lend your support to organizations like The Mountaineers which are continually trying to prevent the flooding and save the valley.

To reach the lake, either take a City Light boat from Diablo Dam or hike down the trail from the North Cascades Highway (see earlier). Rent a boat to visit the valley at the Ross Lake Resort. Make arrangements at the resort to be taken there and picked up later if you'd like to camp.

CAMPGROUNDS (boats only)

Roland Point—2 units, 4 miles north of the dam. Undeveloped.

Rainbow Point—4 units, 5 miles north of dam.

Big Beaver—7 units, 5 miles north of dam.

Lightning Creek—6 units, 12 miles from dam.

Cat Island Camp—7 units, 12 miles with big view of Jack Mountain glaciers.

Little Beaver—7 units, 16 miles from dam, views of Hozomeen Mountain to the northeast.

Other camps at **Silver Creek, Boundary Bay, Ten Mile Island, May Creek** and **Cougar Island.**

Skymo Creek Falls and Ross Lake

I   DARRINGTON

French Creek

First of the National Forest camping areas down the North Fork of the Stillaguamish River. From Arlington, take Highway 530 east. Turn south at sign about 8 miles west of Darrington or 2 miles east of the community of Hazel.

BOULDER CREEK AND FALLS

A level-grade hike of 1 mile through a rich, greenery-draped gorge to a wisp of waterfall pluming from a high cliff into a raging creek.

Drive beyond French Creek Campground on road No. 320 about 2½ miles, watching for a trail sign on the right. Drive a short way down the trail road to park.

Trail follows an old, grown-over road above Boulder Creek. Pass above the first shelter in about ½ mile. Follow the trail above the river to a shelter, nested near huge boulder pools on the creek. The falls lie 200 yards beyond the shelter, draping off the cliff Enchantment Valley style, varying in size with the season. Maintained trail continues 4 miles to the Boulder Ford Camp. A pretty walk as far as you want to go. Huge salmonberries along the trail in season. Trail open some winters.

FRENCH CREEK VIEWS

Look at the valley of the North Fork of the Stillaguamish River and tilted strata of Higgins Mountain on the other side. Follow French Creek road No. 320 and No. 3220 beyond the French Creek Campground up a series of switchbacks. Twisty and steep at first, the road gets better toward the top as it skirts below French Peak and Boulder Ridge.

CAMPGROUNDS

French Creek—30 units in heavy, damp undergrowth of an alder stand. Most units near the creek but screened from it by brush. Picnic area. Pit toilets.

Clear Creek—10 units with 8 designated as trailer units. Sites near the river. But the campground, only 9 miles from Darrington, tends to get heavy town visitor use—night and day. Follow the main street in Darrington (Darrington Street) to the end, turning right along the river to the south.

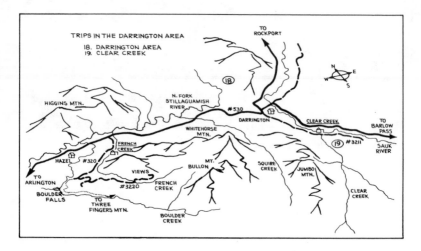

TRIPS IN THE DARRINGTON AREA
18. DARRINGTON AREA
19. CLEAR CREEK

Mount Pugh from Helena Ridge Road

I **DARRINGTON**

Whitehorse Mountain and North Fork Stillaguamish River Valley

18 DARRINGTON AREA

Three logging roads lead to sweeping vistas of the river valleys and snow-covered peaks in the Darrington area.

North Mountain Lookout: A 14-mile drive out of Darrington to expansive views of the Sauk and Suiattle River valleys extending, on clear days, from Puget Sound to Glacier Peak with Mount Baker, Shuksan, White Chuck, White Horse, Bedal, Pugh, and Sloan Peaks thrown in.

Driving out of Darrington, toward Rockport, pass the ranger station and turn 45 degrees left at the swimming pool down a road that runs diagonally through piles of lumber. Follow signs on roads No. 342 and No. 336 to the lookout at 3956 feet.

Segelsen Creek Road: Swiss-type views of the farms in the Stillaguamish valley near Darrington, climbing to vistas that include Glacier, White Chuck, White Horse, Pugh, Sloan, and Bedal Peaks.

Turn north on 187th N.E. (Swede Heaven Road) about 5 miles west of Darrington on Highway 530. Drive about ½ mile after crossing the North Fork of the Stillaguamish River and take a dirt road (forest service road No. 3403) which angles up the hillside. First views in 10 miles. Higher drives bring better views of the nearby peaks. Road continues over ridge to Concrete.

Mine Road: Views of the valley and across to Higgins, plus a short hike to a pretty mountain amphitheater with a waterfall. A great place to picnic.

Turn south on 187th N.E. (Mine Road) about 5 miles west of Darrington. (Same intersection as the Swede Heaven Road.) Drive straight toward White Horse to the end of the road at Snow Gulch. Rough the last ½ mile.

A mine tunnel and tailings at the road end.

To find the amphitheater wander up gravel bars, hopping small creek channels to the base of a cliff. About ¼ mile. Climbers start here on glacier route up White Horse. High water in early summer and avalanche snow in spring may block the way.

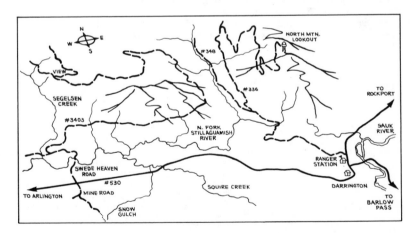

19 CLEAR CREEK

CLEAR CREEK TRAIL

A pleasant ¾-mile path climbs through stately timber high over a Clear Creek gorge.

Find this often unmarked trail across the road from the turnaround loop at the end of the Clear Creek Campground. The path drops off the side of the road and then climbs sharply upward, winding along the edge of the canyon, higher and higher above the creek.

The path ends at a logging road. (An old trail continues to Frog Lake but it is seldom maintained and sometimes impossible to follow.)

Allow enough time for daydreaming and soaking up the beauty of the view into the gorge.

OLD SAUK TRAIL

Hike 3 miles along the banks of the Sauk River—almost any time of year.

Find the trail on the river side of the road No. 3211 about a half-mile upstream from the Clear Creek Campground. Generally signed.

The path follows the river, ending at Murphy Creek.

ASBESTOS CREEK FALLS

Waterfalls from the sky down as Asbestos Creek pours off Jumbo Mountain in a continuous series of cascades.

Take Clear Creek road No. 3210 to the right at the entrance to Clear Creek Campground. The road fords Asbestos Creek in 2 miles. Falls to the right. For better views scramble up the left side of the canyon. Watch for slippery rock.

Stop at Frog Lake on the way back. It's the little pond below the logging road. Entrance road at the lower end. Great place for polliwogs.

HELENA RIDGE ROAD

At 3000 feet, see Mount Baker, Darrington, White Chuck valley, Glacier Peak, Pugh, Bedal, and White Chuck.

Follow the Helena Ridge roads No. 3211 and 3212 past the Clear Creek Campground as they climb swiftly to views from the side of Helena Ridge and Iron Mountain.

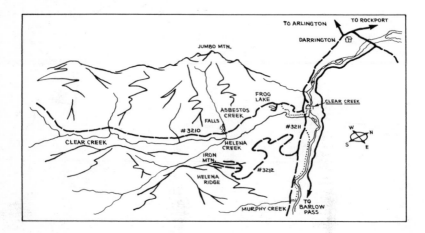

From the Helena Ridge Road

J   SUIATTLE RIVER

A popular access to the Glacier Peak Wilderness. But offering several recreation diversions of its own. Take the paved county road north out of Darrington toward Rockport, turning east in about 6.5 miles onto the Suiattle River road. Road ends at the trailhead into the wilderness area, 26 miles.

BIG CREEK CASCADE

Big Creek plunges down a steep, narrow canyon that many visitors drive over without realizing it even exists. Stop at the first concrete bridge on the Suiattle River road, at about 7 miles. The bridge spans the gorge. Signs of an old washed-out road in the gorge. No trail to the bottom.

CAMPGROUNDS

Buck Creek—50 units, one of the prettiest campgrounds in the state. Sites on both sides of Buck Creek. Two entrances, one on each side of the highway bridge. Some sites near the creek. Others back on timbered loops. All are well-separated in a beautiful stand of timber. Pit toilets. 24 miles from Darrington.

Downey Creek—9 units. Generally undeveloped. Sites on both sides of the creek. First sites near the river. Sites beyond the bridge, on a bluff. Older, primitive area. Pit toilets. 30 miles from Darrington.

Sulphur Creek—26 units. Sulphur Creek splits the campground with most sites near either the creek or the Suiattle River. Pit toilets. 32 miles from Darrington.

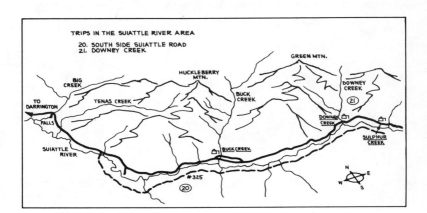

Unnamed waterfall beside road

Suiattle River Valley from Green Mountain Road

20   SOUTH SIDE SUIATTLE ROAD

A pleasant drive but even more a place of remote picnic spots near pleasant creeks.

Turn south across the Suiattle River about 6 miles west of the Buck Creek Campground, turning right at the first junction, following road No. 325 as far as you like.

Watch for dolomite mining claims along the way—white rock similar to marble.

The road crosses a number of small creeks, all headed toward the river. Most of them are worth prowling down on a quiet afternoon.

BUCK CREEK TRAIL

A shady, easy walk through lush timber past roiling big-boulder rapids and deep pools along an unmarked trail north of the Buck Creek Campground.

The trail follows Buck Creek for about ¾ mile before climbing up a lush ridge and then dropping back to the creek. The trail then crosses the creek and ends in the forest. The path once went on to Horse Creek in about 5 miles. Find the path on the west side of the creek just beyond the uppermost campsite.

To hike down to the Suiattle River, find a fisherman's trail on the west side of the creek south of the road. Lots of windfalls to clamber over and under. But the noisy creek will listen to all your complaints.

GREEN MOUNTAIN TRAIL

A steep trail through a mossy forest to one of the largest meadow systems in this area. Overlook the Suiattle River and Downey Creek valleys with Glacier Peak, Box Meadow, and Circle Peaks in the background. Trail reaches meadows at 1½ miles, continuing another 2½ miles to Green Mountain Lookout.

Turn up the Green Mountain road no. 3227 2 miles east of the Buck Creek Campground—the first road beyond the Green Mountain Pasture area. The road starts with views but then winds back through a series of blackened clearcuts.

Drive to the end of the road for clear-day views of Glacier Peak and then backtrack about ¼ mile, finding the marked trail on the uphill side of the road. Sign high on the bank. Don't be fooled by trail mile markers. They were posted before road was built.

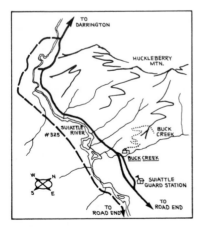

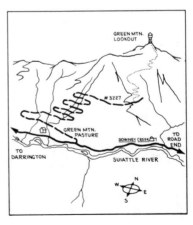

21 DOWNEY CREEK TRAIL

Another pleasant forest walk as far as you want to go.

Find trail on the north side of the road east of Downey Creek. Watch for sign. Trail climbs steeply at first then traverses above the river, returning to river level in about 3 miles. 🏃

SULPHUR CREEK TRAIL

An arboretum of wild greenery along a creek of pools, waterfalls, rocks, and gravel bars.

Find the trail on the left of the Suiattle River road near the Sulphur Creek Campground entrance. It climbs steeply at the start but soon drops down to the creek. Go as far as you like. Trail ends in 2 miles. But all of it is worth a walk. Lots of good picnic spots.

For a side trip, take a spur trail to a sulphur spring. Turn right down a well-worn path at a wilderness sign about .7 miles from the road. The path crosses the creek on a system of flattened footlogs which can be treacherously slippery when wet. Turn upstream, finding the sulphur spring seep, out of a rockslide, in less than 25 yards. 🏃

SUIATTLE RIVER TRAIL

Huge trees, ferns, and nurse logs along two fine forest trails at the end of the Suiattle River road.

Find the trails out of the developed parking area at the end of the road. Follow an abandoned road to the junction of the Milk Creek and Suiattle River trails in about 1 mile.

The Milk Creek trail starts at a bridge over the Suiattle River and climbs almost immediately into rain forest-like growth, gloriously rich with huge trees and understory greenery. A walk of a mile or so leads past tumbling creeks. Turn back when you feel like it.

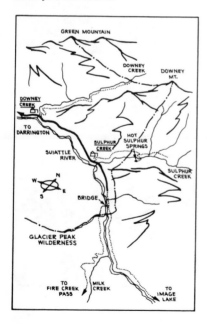

Buck Creek Campground

The Suiattle River trail turns uphill slightly at the junction and plunges into stately forest. In about a ½ mile watch for an unmarked trail back downhill toward the river. It ends at an old shelter and number of sand bars in maybe a quarter-mile. (You can also reach the shelter from the Milk Creek trail bridge by following faint foot paths which pass a fern-covered rock wall of folded schists.)

K   MOUNTAIN LOOP HIGHWAY

Only a few years ago you could wander this once mountain road and really enjoy the trip. But not any more.

Recent improvements took much of the backcountry pleasures out of the road but plans (1977) to turn it into a two-lane paved highway will most certainly destroy them all—forever.

And what's the public cost—beyond the environmental damage? No one will say. But one single bridge in 1977 cost $845,000. So guess what the whole project is likely to run. Several million? More? And will the "improvement" be worth the damage? There may still be time to stop the effort.

MEADOW MOUNTAIN-CRYSTAL LAKE

One used to be able to hike to these places on trails. But now you have to walk down an expensive road that loggers and trailbikers can drive on but you can't.

The Forest Service spent nearly $200,000 of public funds to build this road and put another $79,000 into it during 1977. But still only loggers and trailbikers are now permitted to use it. Other taxpayers must walk.

In the past, you could reach Meadow Mountain by trail in 1½ miles. Now you must walk 4½ miles farther—on the road.

And it was the same with Crystal Lake. A 1-mile hike by trail is now a 3-mile walk, most of it by road.

The reason the Forest Service gives for closing the road, without any prior public notice is to protect the lake and meadows from overuse—brought about by construction of the road. Which makes one wonder why they built it in the first place. Unless, of course, it was simply to subsidize some logger. And does the public really want its money spent that way?

BEAVER LAKE TRAIL

A 2-mile walk over an old abandoned railroad grade leads to a small beaver lake and a haven for wildlife.

Find the trailhead south of the White Chuck Campground near the confluence of the White Chuck and Sauk Rivers and the junction of road No. 322 (Mountain Loop) and the bridge to road No. 3211 on the west side of the Sauk. Trail is generally signed.

Beaver here. Wood ducks, goldeneye, deer and mallards. If you're quiet, of course. And careful.

The trail ends back on the Mountain Loop highway at Lyle Creek. 🚶

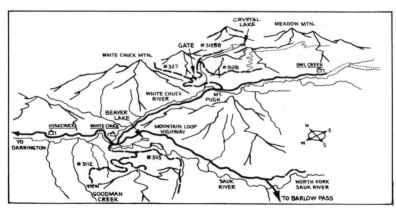

Meadow Mountain Road and Mount Pugh

WHITE CHUCK RIVER ROAD

Easiest route to views of Glacier Peak. Drive 7 miles from the Mountain Loop Highway to a marked viewpoint where Glacier looms at the head of the valley. Views too of White Chuck and Pugh.

FALLS CREEK ROAD

High views of the Sauk River valley, White Chuck, Glacier, Pugh, and Bedal Peaks. Turn west across the Sauk River just south of the White Chuck Campground. In 2 miles, turn west again on Peekaboo road No. 3112. Take all turns to the right. Road ends at Goodman Creek.

CAMPGROUNDS

Hyakchuck—2 units on an unmarked loop road 4 miles from Darrington. Primitive. In forest area east of road. Pit toilet.

White Chuck—10 units. Where the White Chuck River joins the Sauk. Tent and car-camper sites. 11 miles from Darrington. Pit toilets.

Pride Basin and Monte Cristo Peak from road No. 308

L   SAUK RIVER

NORTH FORK FALLS
A roaring torrent less than ¼ mile by trail from North Fork road No. 308. Turn east off the Mountain Loop Highway about 18 miles south of Darrington or 7 miles north of Barlow Pass onto the North Fork road. Drive about a mile. Watch for sign. The steep trail drops from a parking pull-off on the south side of the road. Very slippery when wet.

RED MOUNTAIN VIEWPOINT
A 1-mile hike leads to a viewpoint, once the site of a lookout, with modest views of the North Fork valley of the Sauk including the snow-crested Bedal and Sloan peaks.

Take the Glacier Peak Wilderness trail out of Sloan Creek Campground, finding the Red Mountain trail to the left in about 100 yards just beyond and behind a Forest Service display board.

Trail switchbacks steadily to the lookout site and then continues another ⅛ mile to no better views.

MINERAL SPRINGS

Continue on the wilderness trail out of Sloan Creek Campground past the shelter to the mineral spring, a red-mud area to the left of the trail. Watch for path on left in about 100 yards. 🚶

FOREST WALK

An easy forest walk past awe-inspiring trees in a valley which is now, thankfully, part of the wilderness system.

Take the Glacier Peak Wilderness trail out of Sloan Creek Campground (see above) following it along the river as far as you want. Pleasant forest and huge trees for better than a mile. A magnificent place to forget the pettiness of the city.

HIGH VIEW DRIVE

Follow the North Fork road No. 308 past the Sloan Creek Campground turnoff to clear-day views of the peaks around both Cadet and Sloan Creeks. Take either fork at the "Y" about 2 miles beyond the campground. The road left up Sloan Creek leads to the highest views, looping back above Cadet Creek. See Sloan, Foggy, Monte Cristo, and Cadet Peaks and a large glacier in Pride Basin. Good picnicking. Nice creeks. But watch for logging trucks. 🚗

CAMPGROUNDS

Sloan Creek—7 walk-in units in a beautiful stately old stand of Douglas fir and cedar. Trailhead camp to the Glacier Peak wilderness. Pit toilets. 6 miles from Mountain Loop highway on road No. 308. Watch for sign, campground on a short spur to the left (east).

Bedal—20 units and a shelter. Very pleasant campground—one of the nicest on the Sauk. Some sites on the river. Others on open-timbered ledge overlooking the river. Piped water. Pit toilets. 18 miles from Darrington.

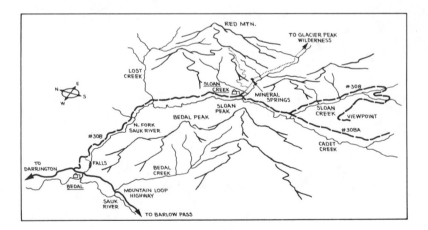

22   SOUTH FORK SAUK RIVER

GOAT LAKE

It's 4½ miles into scenic and popular Goat Lake—well beyond the usual limits set for this book. But a 2-mile walk down the first part of the trail is well worth the effort.

To find the trailhead, drive north on the Mountain Loop Highway turning east on road No. 309 (Elliot Creek) about 4 miles beyond Barlow Pass. The trail starts to the right of a gate.

The path follows Elliot Creek through timber past lots of camping and picnic spots and over sections of old corduroy road. Nearly level most of the way.

The forested path ends on the old road to the old Goat Lake trailhead. But don't return by the road—it's longer, and who wants to walk on a road!

(The trail continues to the old trailhead and then across a logged-over area before returning to forest and climbing to the lake. Camping is limited to formal camp spots at the lake.) 🚶

MONTE CRISTO LAKE

No great spectacles here. No vast stretches of water. But the small ponds invite exploration by kyak and canoe. Not that you'll get lost. Impossible. But you won't be able to avoid the sense of secrecy the place presents.

Find the lakes (ponds?) about 2 miles north of Barlow Pass on the Mountain Loop Highway. One small pond on the right of the road. Others on the left. Water levels vary from year to year and from season to season.

CAMPGROUNDS

Chokwich—11 units, most along the river off a spur road. Alder-conifer stand with undergrowth separating most sites. 20 miles from Darrington. Pit toilets.

South Fork—8 units strung out along the river just off the highway. Some units 15 to 20 yards from the road. Carry your gear in. Pit toilets. 21 miles from Darrington.

Twin Peak and Tyee Pool—3 units at Twin Peak, 3 at Tyee. Sites just off the road next to the river. Pit toilets. 21 miles.

Bedal—18 units near river. 18 miles from Darrington.

Monte Cristo Lake

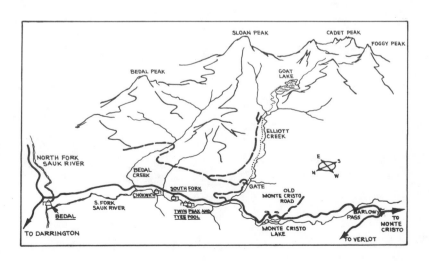

Boardman Lake

M   VERLOT

The Stillaguamish River valley from Verlot to Barlow Pass—with a side trip to the old mining town of Monte Cristo—offers far more than scenery. History, fossil-bearing rock, mountain lakes, and high alpine trails—all in a single area package.

An extremely popular area, crowded—and over-crowded—most summer weekends.

Drive east from Granite Falls. The Verlot District Ranger Station of Mount Baker National Forest in 12.3 miles; Barlow Pass, 33 miles; and Monte Cristo up the South Fork of the Sauk, 38 miles. Or turn north at Barlow Pass and take the Mountain Loop Highway to Darrington.

CAMPGROUNDS

Turlo—19 tent sites in a wooded area across from the Verlot Ranger Station. Some sites near the river. Others on a shaded loop. All well separated. A busy area. Piped water. Vault toilets. A fee camp.

Verlot—24 sites. 10 for tent campers only. The rest for tent or trailer use. Most heavily developed and popular campground in the valley.

Full on weekends. But pleasantly private during the week. Restrooms. Piped water. Fee camp.

Hemple Creek—3 camping sites. 13 picnic-only sites. Fisherman trails and a pool to the east. Piped water. Pit toilets.

Gold Basin—67 sites. 20 for tent campers. The rest for tent or trailer use. Largest campground in the valley. Some sites near the river but most on pleasant wooded loops. Piped water. Pit toilets. Fee camp.

Boardman Camp—8 sites. All along the river. Some walk-in camps. On spur road just beyond Boardman Creek, 6 miles from Verlot. Pit toilets.

Red Bridge—10 sites on a forested bend in the river. Gets heavy trailer use. 8 miles from Verlot. Pit toilets.

River Bar—A gravel bar on the north side of the road across from the Red Bridge Campground. 6 sites for trailers. Pit toilets.

Note: There are a number of smaller camps all along the river near almost every stream. Most are oriented to trailer-camper use. But a few provide tent camping opportunities. Pit toilets at most.

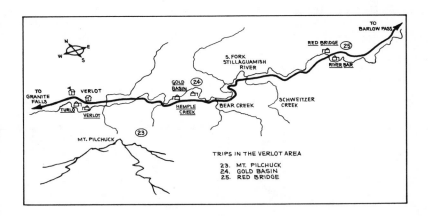

TRIPS IN THE VERLOT AREA

23. MT. PILCHUCK
24. GOLD BASIN
25. RED BRIDGE

23   MOUNT PILCHUCK

A ski area in winter but a popular summer recreation area also.

Turn south onto the Mount Pilchuck road just east of the bridge 1 mile east of the Verlot Ranger Station. Views along the way with the best vista from the ski-lodge area at the end of the road and from the top of the mountain itself.

PILCHUCK LOOKOUT

Vistas here of about everything from Puget Sound and the Olympics to the Cascade peaks.

A steep 2-mile trail leads from the road to the abandoned lookout. Find the trailhead downhill from the ski lodge. The path at the start looks more like a cattle run than a trail; mud and roots several yards wide.

Snow often remains on the trail above timberline until mid-summer or later. Stay on the trail coming down. Seeming shortcuts can be deceptive. Cliffs.

HEATHER LAKE

A 2-mile hike to a cirque lake in subalpine forest and meadow.

Trail leaves the Pilchuck road No. 3014 at 1.5 miles from the valley turnoff, leading up an old logging road at first and into a logged-off area before entering old lovely forest in the valley of Heather Creek. Open meadows in the basin before reaching the lake, at 2450 feet are filling up with little silver firs. No camping within 100 ft. of the lake. Very fragile shore.

LAKE TWENTY-TWO

An extremely popular 2.4 mile trail through a grove of giant cedar and past a series of small waterfalls to a pretty mountain lake (2460) with an almost permanent snowfield at the end. In a Research Natural Area.

Find the trail 2.4 miles east of Verlot Ranger Station on the left (east) side of Twenty-two Creek. No camping and no fires either at the lake or on the trail.

A very popular walk. Up to 500 people a weekend. So don't expect much privacy. And treat the lakeside kindly.

MAIDEN OF THE WOODS

A ¾-mile hike to a wooden lady clinging to the side of a cedar tree in the middle of the forest. Dudley Carter, a Seattle wood sculptor, carved the huge lady for a movie about wood carving.

Turn north on the road No. 3013 east of the Verlot store—watch for the trail sign in about 1½ miles, just after the road turns sharply up a hill. A pleasant trail.

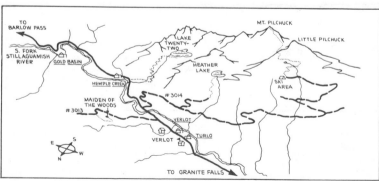

Maiden of the Woods

24 GOLD BASIN

GOLD BASIN SLIDE
Across from Gold Basin Campground. Blue-gray silts and clays deposited centuries ago in the bottom of a lake formed when the valley was dammed by glacial ice just below the slide area. Some pan for gold in the river near the slide.

BLACK CREEK LOG DAM
No trail but a fairly easy ½-mile scramble to a rare example of a high log dam built to supply waterpower to a sawmill, since collapsed and overgrown.

Start at the west end of the rock bridge over Black Creek ½ mile from the Gold Basin Campground. Veer right into open timber, away from the creek, then work upstream along a series of benches always keeping the creek within earshot. Signs of old trail, pipes, wire, collapsed buildings, and puncheon along the way.

Either view the dam from above through the trees or else scramble up the creek the last 50 or so yards. Signs of the old sawmill south of the highway about 100 yards west of the bridge. Use care in climbing over the rotten structure.

Schweitzer Creek Road
A single logging road with high views over the Stillaguamish River valley leads to trails to four mountain lakes. Turn south on the first logging road east of the Gold Basin Campground—Schweitzer Creek road No. 3015. At the junction, about 2.8 miles, keep left, road No. 3015, to trails to Evan and Boardman Lakes; right, road No. 3015B, to trails to Bear and Pinnacle.

EVAN AND BOARDMAN LAKES
An easy trail of about 1 mile leads first past Evan Lake and then climbs gradually through timber to Boardman. Trail gets sloppy when wet.

Evan Lake—A 12-acre lake at 2981 feet only a few hundred yards from the road. Watch for trail sign on the left after the road makes a sharp switchback to the right about 2 miles from the junction. Shallow, weedy shoreline.

Boardman Lake—A pretty 50-acre lake at 3370 feet, surrounded by big timber and rock bluffs. The trail reaches the lake near the inlet. Camping on a bench above the lake.

BEAR AND PINNACLE LAKES
A smooth, level trail—crested and finished with crushed rock—leads to Bear Lake in less than ½ mile. But it takes a low-gear, tedious, sometimes sloppy 2-

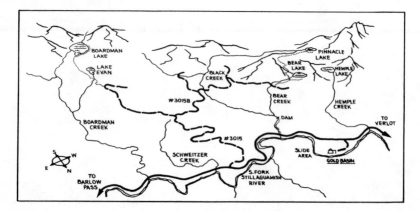

Devil's club

mile effort to reach the alpine Pinnacle Lake.

   Bear Lake—A path—it's much too posh to be called a trail—leads along the edge of a clear cut—turn right at the junction to a timbered lake at 2775 feet. Push a baby carriage down it if you like. An expansive but undeveloped area near the lake for picnicking. Heavily used. Fisherman's paths around most of the lake.

   Pinnacle Lake—Turn left at the junction. Posh path for another ½ mile gives way to a sloppy forest trail. Occasional views down on Bear Lake and over the valley break up the tedium of the climb. Trail tops out across a series of marshy flower-huckleberry meadows to reach the lake at 3820 feet surrounded by patches of timber, steep meadows, and scenic rock bluffs. 1.7 miles from road. Do not camp near lake.

25   RED BRIDGE

Black Chief Mine

An old mine tunnel extends 125 feet into a mountain only a few yards off the highway. Mine entrance through the trees across from the Red Bridge Campground just east of the Red Bridge. In the northeast quadrant of the road junction. The mine was abandoned in 1926 after no ore had been found in an operation begun in the early 1900s. The shaft is not timbered. 🚙

MONTE CRISTO RAILROAD

Old pilings and occasional signs of an old roadbed cut are all that's left of the railroad that once ran as far as Monte Cristo.

Best signs of piling can be seen in the river at Boardman Creek and just off the highway through the trees to the south at the gravel section (washout) in the road west of Silverton.

Parts of the old roadbed are visible at Big Four, Barlow Pass, and along the road to Monte Cristo. All the old tunnels have been plugged. 🚙

GOLD PANNING

No promises, now. But some campers have been seen panning for gold along the upper reaches of the river, particularly in the Gold Basin and Red Bridge Campground areas. Some of the smaller streams also attract an occasional prospector.

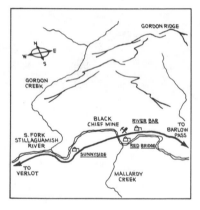

Cascades golden-mantled ground squirrel

Skunk cabbage near Silverton

Big Four Mountain from Coal Creek Road

N   SILVERTON TO MONTE CRISTO

CAMPGROUNDS

Coal Creek—4 sites. Tables. Fire pits. But no toilets. Generally undeveloped. But with spectacular views of Big Four Mountain from the gravel bar along the river. 13 miles from Verlot.

Upper Sauk—From Barlow Pass to Monte Cristo. No established camps but a number of primitive areas beside the river. No facilities. No fee. Pick your own.

Monte Cristo—3 primitive sites with a view up the valley. Steep, narrow road prevents trailer use. Pit toilet. 23 miles from Verlot.

Note: There are a number of smaller very attractive camps along the South Fork of the Sauk between Barlow Pass and Monte Cristo. Most are trailer and camper oriented. But there are some good tent sites too.

Sauk River trout

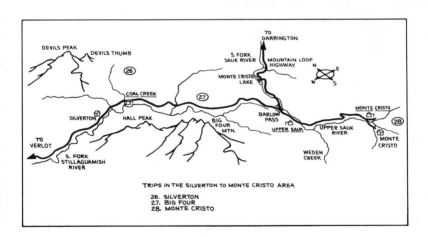

TRIPS IN THE SILVERTON TO MONTE CRISTO AREA

26. SILVERTON
27. BIG FOUR
28. MONTE CRISTO

26   SILVERTON

Abandoned lead, silver, and gold mines. Less than 1 mile by trail from the old mining town of Silverton—now the site of summer homes.

Turn south across the bridge at Silverton—12 miles east of Verlot—following the narrow street straight ahead until it ends in a couple of blocks. Trail off a stub road to the right in about 25 yards. To the left.

(If street is chained just at the other side of the bridge, park on the road and walk in. Only a couple of blocks farther.)

Trail follows a grown-over wagon road to the first of three mines between the 2000- and 2425-foot levels. Scramble up tailing piles to the left of the trail where it cuts past a collapsed shed and machinery. Old tunnel at the top on the right side of a canyon. Trails to other mines are not marked. Search them out for yourself.

Tunnels have not been maintained or timbered for years. Most are in a state of collapse. Some extend as far as 1600 feet back into the mountain. All are private property.

BIG FOUR VIEW

Walk—don't drive—down an old logging road to a sweeping vista of the upper river valley and Big Four Mountain.

Turn north on Deer Creek road No. 3016 about 1 mile east of Silverton. Turn right at the first junction, walking down the spur road beyond a gate. The road is often closed because of "logging hazards."

Best views as the road starts switchbacking up hill. Even better at the very end. Leaf imprint rocks can sometimes also be found in the road cut at the very end.

KELCEMA LAKE

About ½ mile by easy trail that starts near the end of logging road No. 3016. Watch for sign and parking area on the left. A mountain cirque lake on the north side of Bald Mountain.

Drive north on Deer Creek road No. 3016, turning left at the junction within a mile. Trailhead in about another 3 miles.

A heavily used area. Don't camp near the lake. Best camping across the log jam at the outlet.

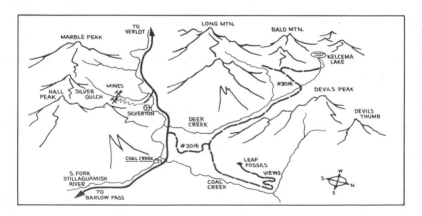

Big Four Mountain and South Fork Stillaguamish River

27   BIG FOUR

Site of an old resort in what was once advertised as the "Alps of America." Ruins of an old fireplace and concrete powerhouse are all that is left of the complex that almost filled the flat. Drive 15 miles east of Verlot. Watch for the Big Four sign.

ICE CAVES

Caves in snowfields at the base of Big Four Mountain about 1 mile by trail from a picnic area on the site of the old Big Four resort. Number and size of the caves vary from year to year.

The trail starts directly from the parking area at Big Four (find sign) and heads toward the Stillaguamish River over an old concrete sidewalk, part of the original resort complex. A new big bridge fords the river and the trail continues through pleasant forest to the base of the Big Four cliffs and the sun-sheltered snow fields.

One warning. The caves are not usually open until mid-July or later and can be hazardous, as can the snow above them. So explore with extreme care. Call Verlot Ranger Station to find out conditions in advance.

BEAVER DAMS

The flats around Big Four and on both sides of the highway are prime beaver country. But locations of beaver dams vary from year to year. Each explorer must seek his own.

INDEPENDENCE AND COAL LAKES

Drive past one to hike to another. Both pretty mountain lakes. Turn north beyond Big Four on road No. 3006. Big views of the valley and Big Four Mountain at a viewpoint, 2.2 miles. And look for leaf-imprint rocks in the road cut behind the formal vista display.

Coal Lake—About 50 yards off the road to the right. Watch for sign. An easy canoe or kayak carry. No power boats here. A few camping spots on the south shore. A narrow snowfed lake of 64 acres at 3420 feet surrounded by steep timber and rock slopes.

Independence Lake—Worth every step of the ¾-mile trail. Drive to the end of the road. Trail climbs through a clear cut and then drops into timber down one of the branches of Coal Creek before climbing up sharply to the lake at 3700 feet. Noisy little falls at the outlet.

Hike around the south side of the crystal blue lake to the open meadow at the inlet end. Camping off the meadows in the timber.

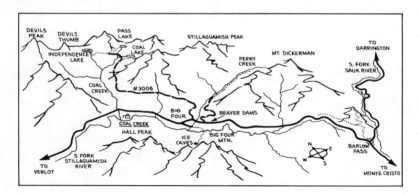

Beaver dam near Big Four Campground

BARLOW LOOKOUT SITE

A 1-mile switchback trail to modest views of Big Four, Dickerman, and Sheep Mountains, Monte Cristo Lakes, and the Stillaguamish valley. Lots of mushrooms on lower levels in the fall.

Trail starts at Barlow Pass, skirting the south side of the ridge above the highway on the old government trail before turning up the mountain in a series of switchbacks through timber to the viewpoint.

The old government trail—which was the early day route over Barlow Pass to Monte Cristo—continues downhill a total of 3 miles. In timber mostly.

28   MONTE CRISTO

A one-time booming mining town, now an off-and-on resort.

Old buildings, remnants of power flumes, a railway turntable and scattered heaps of rusting mine machinery are about all that remain of the once busy community. All on private land. Access by auto may be gated. 🚗

GLACIER BASIN

It's a scramble to get there. But the spectacle is hard to beat! 2.1 miles.

Find the trail out of the Monte Cristo Forest Service campground near the end of the road to Monte Cristo. To reach the campground follow an uphill spur to the left before the road crosses a bridge into the Monte Cristo complex.

The trail follows an old jeep road for about 1 mile and then scrambles sharply upward another mile along an old iron flume to a waterfall and then to a valley marred by mine operations. Continue to the spectacular alpine cirque at the end.

Don't camp on the meadows here. Find spots on the ridges, up in the rocks or on Ray's Knoll. Heavy use is rapidly destroying the place. 🚶

SILVER LAKE

A steep and sloppy 2-mile trail climbs Poodle Dog Pass to a heather-meadow lake on the south side of the ridge above the resort. The trail starts at the end of a spur road uphill, to the right, just beyond the bridge into the Monte Cristo area. The path climbs sharply through open areas with views of the valley. Just beyond the pass a long, rough trail turns left to Twin Lakes. Trail to the right drops down to Silver Lake. 🚶

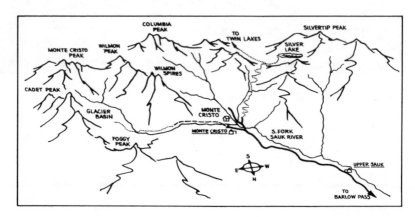

Wilmon Peak above Monte Cristo

Skykomish River

O   INDEX TO STEVENS PASS

Spur roads off busy Stevens Pass Highway 2 lead to lakes, waterfalls, mine areas, high meadows, and quiet forest trails.

Drive east from Monroe through Sultan, Startup, and Goldbar.

MOUNTAIN VIEWS

Vistas opening with Mounts Index and Baring and ending with sweeping high views to the high peaks in the Monte Cristo area.

Turn north off Highway 2 onto paved Rieter road about 1½ miles east of Goldbar. In less than a mile take rough, gravel road No. 2708 straight ahead where the paved road turns sharply left.

Mount Index views over the Skykomish River valley in about 5 miles. Views of the North Fork valley, Kyes and Columbia Peaks of the Monte Cristo group, and Gunn and Baring between the forks of the Skykomish—in 10 miles.

BARCLAY LAKE

A mile-long walk to a pleasant lake along a trail that raises serious questions about the Forest Service's "recreation" values.

First of all the trail starts in an ugly clear cut—take care to note how "quickly" (?) it's regrowing to a new forest. Notice then how the Forest Service permitted logging for a ways right up to the trail. Then notice how the logging keeps moving away from the trail—about a foot at a time with each new sale—until—finally—the hiker can enjoy the forest without the desolation of a "sustained yield harvest."

The lake, tucked beneath the towering shadow of Baring mountain, offers lots of picnic and camping spots in which to contemplate what you've seen. And even, thankfully, forget it.

Turn north off Highway 2 about 6 miles from Index onto Baring road No. 278. Find trail downhill to the left, before the road ends, in about 4½ miles. Watch for signs and garbage cans.

CAMPGROUNDS

Troublesome Creek—24 sites. Most of the sites along the North Fork of the Skykomish and Troublesome Creek. Sites both east and west of the bridge, in old-growth Douglas fir and hemlock. Pit toilets. 10 miles north of Index.

San Juan—12 campsites along the river in shaded hardwood area. A pleasant camp. Pit toilets. 12 miles from Index.

Beckler River Camp—12 developed sites in an open, gravel second-growth area. Some sites near the river, a few in the shade. Pit toilets. 1 mile north of Skykomish.

Money Creek—19 sites, some near the river, some on forest loops. Part of the camp in open timber. Some in undergrowth. A busy camp just off the highway. Pit toilets. Piped water. 4 miles west of Skykomish. Fee camp.

Miller River—16 units in old-growth timber area. All on forested loops. Pit toilets. 3.2 miles south of Highway 2.

Foss River—5 sites near the Foss River in a wooded area. Pit toilets. Gets heavy hiker use. Near trailhead to Trout Lake.

Tye Canyon—A pleasant but primitive camp—one table only—off the Tye Canyon road about ½ mile east of the Martin Creek bridge. Places to camp in timber. One on the river. Generally full on weekends. Pit toilets.

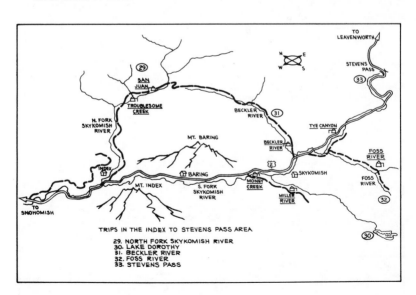

TRIPS IN THE INDEX TO STEVENS PASS AREA
29. NORTH FORK SKYKOMISH RIVER
30. LAKE DOROTHY
31. BECKLER RIVER
32. FOSS RIVER
33. STEVENS PASS

29   NORTH FORK SKYKOMISH RIVER

The first section—Index to Jack Pass—of a loop drive that starts from Highway 2 at Index, circles north, returning to the highway at Skykomish. 45 miles round trip. 28.8 miles, Index to Skykomish. Road paved almost 12 miles.

SILVER CREEK MINES
A rough road, not recommended for passenger cars and sometimes closed, leads up Silver Creek canyon past several old mine workings. Broken Ridge Copper Mine in 1½ miles. Watch for tunnels and signs of workings just off the road on the left.

Other workings farther on. None maintained. Most in a state of collapse. Some closed or blocked inside by slides. Can be dangerous!

Cross the North Fork about 2 miles west of Troublesome Creek Campground, taking the fork right on the other side of the bridge. Drive as far as you can. Mineral City in 4.5 miles. An old mining area with no structures left. 🚐

TROUBLESOME CREEK TRAIL
What was once an old miner's trail is now a busy—and pretty—interpretive trail along and around a tumbling creek.

Find the trail under the bridge out of the Troublesome Creek campground on the west side of the creek. The path winds upstream past stately old-growth Douglas fir and along a tumble of cascades to a bridge. Cross the creek and return to the road on a trail that climbs through forest to still other views of the creek. 🚶

BEAR CREEK FALLS
A squat torrent that pours out of a rock gap into a beautiful pool. Less than ¼ mile from the road.

Trail drops off the south side of the road about 1 mile east of Troublesome Creek bridge. Watch for a small turnoff where the trail drops through trees on a curve. No formal sign.

Trail leads to rock outcropping below the falls. Watch your footing when rocks are wet. 🚶

SAN JUAN FALLS
During the spring and fall, a pretty falls about ½ mile east of the San Juan Campground. A part-time stream tumbles off a high rock bluff on the south side of the road. A thin trickle in summer. Flows best during high-water seasons. 🚐

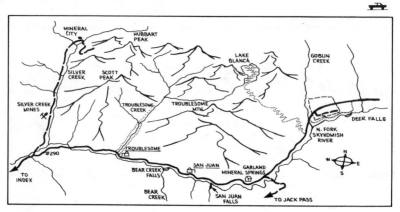

Mount Index, left, and Mount Persis, right, from Stevens Pass Highway

GARLAND MINERAL SPRINGS

An occupied but inoperative resort on private land at the head of the North Fork valley about 3 miles east of Troublesome Creek Campground and only a few miles below Jack Pass.

Property now includes several old cabins, a handful of out-buildings, and an empty swimming pool. Watch for unmarked rock-rimmed soda springs near the entrance road, to the east. Signs of rusty seeps in other areas. Lukewarm water with a high mineral-salty taste.

DEER FALLS

North Fork of the Skykomish River drops 70 feet over a slab cliff. Highest falls in the North Fork area and a good place to wonder about Forest Service recreation policy.

Take North Fork road No. 290 east from Garland Hot Springs (be sure to bear left at Jack Pass junction) driving 3.2 miles to Goblin Creek. About .2 mile beyond creek, turn right toward river down logging road, bearing left at the bottom of the hill.

Find the trail off the road, as it starts paralleling the creek, by picking your way through logging debris toward the river. Walk downstream about .4 mile to the falls. You'll hear the roar.

But as important as the falls, note how this area was logged. The trail at one time wandered through stately forest to the falls. The walk itself was worthwhile! And then the Forest Service decided to make it "less hazardous" but still "undisturbed" by conducting what it euphemistically called a "sanitation-salvage" timber sale.

You judge. It's a shambles. A mess. An insult to the falls and all of the people who would like to see it. ⚊

Lake Dorothy

30   LAKE DOROTHY

The biggest alpine lake and one of the most beautiful on the west side of the Cascade Crest. 1½ miles through pleasant forest and past a junction of waterfalls from the end of the Miller River road.

At 3052 feet, the lake, dotted with small rocky islands, stretches 2 miles down a long alpine-timbered valley. Trail touches the outlets (good views here) and then skirts the steep east side of the lake before turning westward, across the marshy south end of the lake, and climbing toward Bear, Deer and Snoqualmie Lakes (another 2 miles).

Take at least two snacks on this easy walk. Eat the first at the waterfall-filled stream junction at the footbridge about ⅔ of the way. Save the rest for the lake. Picnic spots at the outlet. Best camping farther down the trail near the lake.

Turn south off Highway 2 about 4 miles west of Skykomish—watch for Money Creek Campground signs. Turn south again in about 1 mile onto Miller River Road. Drive to the end. Lots of parking. 9.3 miles from Highway 2.

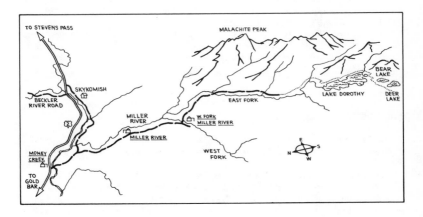

31   BECKLER RIVER

Eastern half of the loop drive into the mountains from Index to Skykomish. Jack Pass to Highway 2, 12.5 miles.

JACK PASS
Expansive views of the North Fork valley and the Monte Cristo area peaks including Twin, Columbia, and Kyes.

Take road No. 2860 west out of the Jack Pass complex, keeping right at the first fork, No. 2860A. Viewpoint in less than a mile. Continuing views out over the valley and into the North Fork Skykomish River area on the road from Jack Pass to Garland Mineral Springs. 🚗

EVERGREEN MOUNTAIN
Hike only 1½ miles to one of the most spectacular clear-day views in this section of the Cascades.

Trail takes off at the end of the road, switchbacks up a clear cut and partially burned ridge, traverses an unburned area and then bursts suddenly, in the last half mile, into open flower-filled meadows.

Lookout tower (5585) at the top with 360 degree views of Glacier Peak, Mount Rainier and the Monte Cristo peaks. But wander a way down the ridge on an abandoned trail for a private lunch spot with your own private view. Bring your water.

Drive south from Jack Pass, taking the lower East Beckler road No. 280. Evergreen road No. 285 turns east in about 1 mile, crossing Evergreen Creek before starting its climb, first to the south and then switching back to the north. Take the first spur to the right, No. 285A, beyond the switchback to reach the trailhead and parking area. Big views, even from the road. 🚗 🚶

BECKLER PEAK
Drive to about 3000 feet for views of most of the major peaks in the Stevens Pass-Skykomish area.

Turn north off Highway 2 onto the Beckler Peak road No. 263 2½ miles east of the Beckler River road, 2 miles from the new Skykomish District Ranger Station.

Striking views of Mount Baring as the road climbs westward. The vista expands as the road switchbacks to the east with open views of the Tye River valley, the Hinman Glacier on Mount Hinman, Mount Daniels, Surprise, and other peaks of the Cascade Crest.

Watch for logging traffic, even on weekends. 🚗

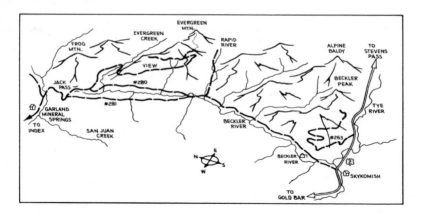

Foss River Valley from Beckler Peak Road

Mountaineers clean Trout Lake

32   FOSS RIVER

TONGA RIDGE ROAD

A high mountain road offering continually changing vistas of the major peaks in the Stevens Pass area.

Turn south off Highway 2 on the first road east of the new Skykomish District Ranger Station, about ½ mile. Keep right at road No. 2622, turning east onto road No. 2605 at the Y, 3.2 miles.

At 6.9 miles from Highway 2, views of Hinman Glacier, Mt. Daniel, the Necklace Valley area, and the West Fork of the Foss River. At 8.3 miles: Mount Index, Mount Baring, Eagle Rock, Glacier Peak, and Beckler River drainage. At 10.3 miles add Mount Fernow to all the rest. Road reaches 3850 feet at highest point. ▭

TONGA RIDGE TRAIL

In less than 1½ miles, grass meadows at 4000 feet along Tonga Ridge with views sweeping from Glacier Peak south through the glaciers on Mt. Hinman.

Turn south off the Tonga Ridge road No. 2605 about 6.8 miles from the Y (see above). Watch for signs. Trail at the end of the spur road climbs through brush onto the open ridge and highest views in the section. Mount Sawyer in 2½ miles. ⋏

TROUT LAKE

A moderately steep trail to a small lake at 2102 feet and past one of the biggest trees in Snoqualmie National Forest. 1½ miles.

Trail leads through an old mine area past remnants of pipelines and mining equipment. Tunnel in brush and timber above the trail. Unmarked. The biggest tree—a 12-foot Douglas fir—marked next to the trail, about 1 mile.

Trail at end of road No. 2622. ⋏

MALONEY RIDGE VIEWS

Site of a microwave tower with views north over the highway and of the Cascade Crest, including Glacier and Hinman again.

Turn west at the Y off the Foss River road to road No. 2504. Tower complex 9.6 miles from Highway 2. It may be necessary to park on the logging road and walk to the viewpoint just beyond the microwave station. ▭

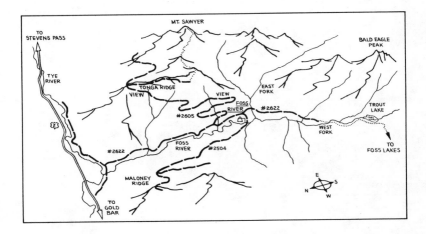

Deception Falls

33   STEVENS PASS

DECEPTION FALLS

A roadside falls about 2 miles west of Scenic on Highway 2. Parking and restrooms on the north side of the busy highway. Falls on the south side.

Find a short spur trail to two more falls downstream from the parking lot. Noises of the highway disappear in a quiet stand of old growth timber. 🚗

TYE CANYON ROAD

A pleasant respite from the rushing highway. A 3-mile winding drive through timber alongside the tumbling Tye River.

Turn north on road No. 2607 just west of Scenic and the main highway bridge across the Tye. Road wends westward along the north side of the river, rejoining the highway just west of the Alpine Falls. The old Stevens Pass Highway. 🚗

RAILWAY RUINS

The west entrance of the abandoned Great Northern railroad tunnel, snow-shed, and townsite of Wellington just off the old Stevens Pass Highway.

Take the old highway north off Highway 2 just west of the summit, turning off to the right onto a gravel spur road at the bottom of the switchbacks—watch for what appears to be a gravel pit operation on the right.

Old tunnel entrance about 50 yards to the left off the spur road. Watch for it through the brush. If the tunnel is open, walk a short way into it for faint glimmers of light from the eastern entrance.

Old townsite of Wellington—renamed Tye by the railroad the day after 96 train passengers were killed in a nearby avalanche—lies between the tunnel entrance and snowshed, and to the north.

Hike down the old railroad through the snowsheds for further views of the valley. About 1½ miles to Windy Point tunnel. Way is washed out in spots, rough, and brushy. 🚗

SKYLINE LAKE

A steep 1¼-mile trail to a small but pretty alpine lake set in open heather-huckleberry meadows at 4950 feet.

Take the narrow road north on the west side of the service station at the summit. Park in the summit parking area. No place to park up the narrow road. Walk past a handful of summer homes, following a bulldozer track to a Highway Department relay station, 1 mile. Dozer track continues another ¼ mile to the lake. Private land. 🚶

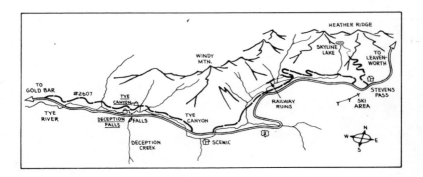

Bathing rocks on Denny Creek

P   SNOQUALMIE PASS

Waterfalls, rock forms, nature trails, hot springs, and high views—all practically at the edge of town.

Drive east from Seattle on I-5 past North Bend, taking side roads up the Middle Fork of the Snoqualmie River, Taylor River, and Denny Creek. Snoqualmie Pass, 24 miles east of North Bend.

Campgrounds here are generally full throughout the summer. But there's always hiking room on trails and side roads.

CAMPGROUNDS

Denny Creek—60 units on a series of loops with 12 or so near the river, the rest in timber. A very busy, heavily used campground particularly on weekends. Pit toilets.

Taylor River—30 sites on a bar formed by the Middle fork of the Snoqualmie River and Taylor River. A timbered area with undergrowth of vine maple and alder. Some sites near the rivers. Others back from the streams. All off several spurs near the entrance. Pit toilets.

Undeveloped Camps—Camping at undeveloped sites along the Middle Fork is restricted to those formally signed and designated for camping. Camps start at forest boundary and continue to the end of the road at Hardscrabble Creek.

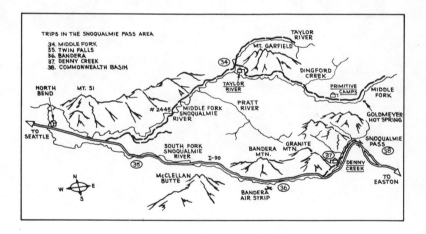

Middle Fork Snoqualmie River and Mount Garfield

34   MIDDLE FORK

Delicate stone forms near a campground and a trail that climbs to open views of mountains in the Alpine Lakes area—all off the road up the Middle Fork of the Snoqualmie River.

Drive east past North Bend on I-90 turning right at the Edgewick Interchange No. 34 looping north onto road No. 2445. In about 15 miles, on what may be one of the roughest roads in Western Washington, follow road No. 241 east over the Taylor River and then up the Middle Fork again.

Note: The Taylor River road No. 240 is expected to remain closed at least until an Alpine Lakes management plan, which will include the road area, has been completed. And it may be that the road will not be opened again. ⊞

CLAYSTONE FORMS

Small, oddly-rounded limestone forms found along the Taylor River. Some resemble small animals while others look more like first-grader experiments in clay. None look alike.

Called concretions, the small forms were created through a lengthy process in which dissolved limestone was deposited around particles of rock or fossil in beds of blue clay laid down in lakes at the front of the ancient Puget Glacier.

Find the small forms in the sharp rocks along the Taylor River starting about 100 yards north of the Taylor River Campground. Look closely for any small round form. Some even look, at first, like sticks. Most are covered with a slick layer of brown silt. Once you've found one, however, the others come easier. The supply is more plentiful the farther you get away from camp. 🚶 ⊞

MIDDLE FORK TRAIL

Walk first through valley forests and then through more open places with views out at peaks in the Alpine Lakes Area. 2 miles or as far and high as you want to go.

Find the trail at the end of road No. 241 about 12 miles from the Taylor River crossing. Parking area and trailhead at the end of the road.

The trail climbs along the river higher and higher reaching vistas up at Iron Cap Mountain, Summit Chief and others in this scenic area.

The path continues to Dutch Miller Gap in 7 miles. The trail, part of the Cascade Crest system (1977), is to be bypassed by a new section in the Crest system. 🚶

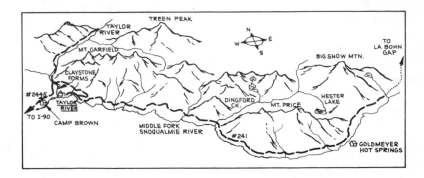

Lower Twin Falls

35 TWIN FALLS

Two spectacular waterfalls just a few hundred feet off a rushing highway. But you can't see them anymore. In fact, you may never see them again.

Before I-90 was constructed you could stop alongside the highway east of North Bend and walk through pleasant forest to look down on the falls and the huge eroded bowls scooped out of the stream walls. Spectacular!

But the concrete experts, the great highway builders, the engineers who spend enormous sums of your money to "improve" your lot blocked the access (after all nothing must stop the rushing auto) while other agencies simply stood by.

Yes, the falls are on state park land. And yes, the State Department of Parks and Recreation—someday—may find enough money to build a new trail to the falls from below (actually, they'd like some private group to do the job—as a civic project).

So when you drive now from North Bend toward Snoqualmie Pass and top the big grade west of town, wonder about what you're missing. And about the value of "progress". And concrete.

36 BANDERA

Short drives up logging roads on either side of I-90 west of Snoqualmie Pass lead to big views of the Snoqualmie River Valley and its bordering mountain ridges.

Lookout road No. 2218A: Turn right off I-90 at the Bandera Interchange looping north to road No. 2218. Bear left following the logging road westward as it traverses upward. 3 miles to a switchback, the end of the road and a parking area.

Walk 1.3 miles eastward and upward, to views of Snoqualmie valley, McClellan Butte, the top of Mount Rainier and, on clear days, the Olympics. Scrambles up the hillside to even fuller views.

Camp Joy road No. 2218: Turn right off Lookout road (see above) about ½ mile from I-90, driving uphill about 3.2 miles to modest views of South Fork valley and over the freeway.

Hansen Creek road No. 2291: Turn right (south) off I-90 at the Denny Creek Interchange. Drive back westerly on road No. 222, taking the Hansen Creek road to the left in about 2 miles. Follow the road, keeping left again at the "Y", onto a spur with view of Bandera, Granite, and Snoqualmie Pass peaks. The road is gated at the top (Seattle watershed).

Asahel Curtis Nature Trail: Follow a pleasant ¾-mile trail through an old-growth stand of Douglas fir, western red cedar, hemlock and noble fir just off the freeway. Find the trail off the Forest Service parking area south of I-90 at the Denny Creek Interchange. A new path under the freeway leads to a picnic area.

The grove of old-growth trees was named after Asahel Curtis, an early-day naturalist, photographer and conservationist who played an active role in the preservation of such places.

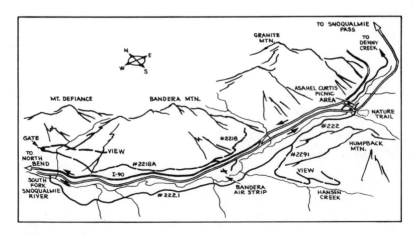

37   DENNY CREEK

Leave the rush of the freeway for a pocket of quiet just below Snoqualmie Pass. Turn off I-90 about 17 miles from North Bend at the Denny Creek Interchange, driving about 2 miles to the Denny Creek Campground. 🚌

FRANKLIN FALLS

Hike here and measure for yourself the cost of progress. Compare the past beauty of this 70-foot plume of water, draped with late afternoon rainbows and rimmed by forests, with its setting today below the "improvement" of a freeway.

An easy 1½-mile walk above the Denny Creek Campground. Start either at the campground or near the bridge across the river above the camp.

The trail passes behind several summer homes and then climbs above the river with views into a series of rapids in a steep, narrow gorge. Trail ends below the falls—and highway. 🚶

WAGON TRAIL

Long before automobiles wobbled over the rocks of Snoqualmie Pass, wagons made the trip down roads that were even worse. One section of the original wagon road near the campground is being preserved in a project undertaken by Chief Seattle Boy Scout Council.

First section of the road starts directly opposite the turnoff onto the road across the bridge above the campground. Look for the wagon wheel display on the east side of the road. The trail is cleared to Franklin Falls. 🚶

BATHING ROCKS

A pleasant walk on a sunny, summer day to basking places on water-washed rock slabs in Denny Creek. The creek fans out over smooth rock chutes to provide places in which even small children can play.

Hike less than 1½ miles to the second crossing of Denny Creek on the Denny Creek trail to Melakwa Lake. After a rest, walk another half mile for a view of Keekwulee Falls.

Find the trail out of the campground or from a parking lot north of the campground. To reach the parking lot drive north from the campground turning left across a bridge. Lot at the end of the spur road. Trail is signed. 🚶

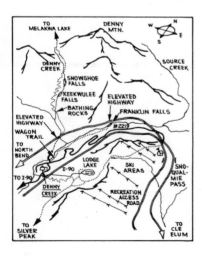

Lodge Lake and Denny Mountain

LODGE LAKE

The noise of the big trucks on I-90 yields to silence on the timbered shores of Lodge Lake less than a ½-mile—as the decibels travel—from the highway.

Find the Cascade Crest trailhead in a wooded area off a parking lot east of Snoqualmie Pass ski area. The trail starts in timber, crosses a section of ski slope and then passes Beaver Lake before entering timber again and climbing to Lodge Lake and beyond. 2½ miles.

The Mountaineers built its first lodge (hence the name) at the lake in 1914. It burned in the late 1930s. Skiing and climbing in the vicinity got their start as a result of lodge activity.

38   COMMONWEALTH BASIN

A 2-mile walk leads into a peaceful forest with glimpses of mountain tops through the trees. Add another mile and gain clearer views from the trail to Red Mountain Pass.

Find the trailhead on the right off the Alpental Road near Commonwealth Creek about ½ mile from the first stop sign after leaving the freeway.

The trail starts in forest, crossing several clear cuts and following a logging road before reaching the edge of the basin in about ¾ mile. From a crossing of Commonwealth Creek in about 1¼ miles, the trail climbs over a shoulder on Kendall Peak and then drops to the valley floor again at the end of 2 miles.

For better views, hike another mile—or less—up the switchbacks leading to Red Mountain. The heather gardens in the basin at the foot of Red Mountain await those who go clear to the top of the pass. ⩕

SNOW LAKE

A longer walk here than most others in this book. But so popular it cannot be ignored, even by the novice. 4 miles one way, so allow all day.

Find the trail off a parking lot at the end of the Alpental Road about 2 miles from the first stop sign after you leave the freeway (see above).

The trail climbs gradually through forest and across open slopes above Source Creek, making its way to a point above little Source Lake before switchbacking through alpine slopes to a saddle in about 3½ miles. Stop here if you like, certainly to rest. The trail drops to the lake in another ½ mile.

A busy place on weekends. But picnic spots abound. Don't leave any trash—even though lots of others have. ⩕

HYAK FOREST ROAD

For view up Gold Creek to Rampart and Chikamin Ridges take the rough forest road that climbs through the Hyak Ski Area.

Best views from the top of the ridge. However, the road continues another 2½ miles along the power line.

Find the road near the Hyak Ski Area parking lot. 🚐

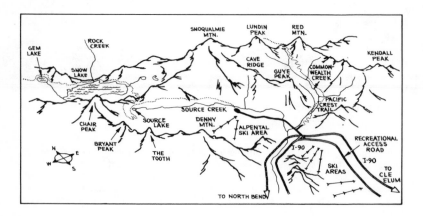

Commonwealth Basin and Red Mountain

From Lookout Mountain near Twisp

Q   THE EAST SLOPE

Sunshine and sagebrush, certainly. But much, much more: High mountains, crisp ridges, waterfalls, rushing rivers, quiet valleys and breathtaking vistas. With all of them to be found on the eastern slope of the Cascade range from just south of Ellensburg to the Canadian border.

Snoqualmie Pass, Stevens Pass and the North Cascades Highway lead to the edges of this expansive countryside.

From Snoqualmie Pass, main highways lead into the high country of Cle Elum River, the Taneum and the Teanaway. From Stevens Pass, other roads lead to the enormous Wenatchee recreation area, the Icicle, the Swauk, and north to Entiat, Chelan and the even higher roads of Harts Pass and the Pasayten.

As always, roads are only the beginning. The best, certainly, is reserved for the hiker willing to wander any of the hundreds of trails that leave campgrounds, road ends and waysides for lookouts, lakes, waterfalls—the natural lot.

The outdoor season on this side of the Cascades is a little longer than on the west side of the range. Spring comes sooner; fall, a little later. Summers, though, are hotter and winters, colder, with both varying year to year, as you would expect.

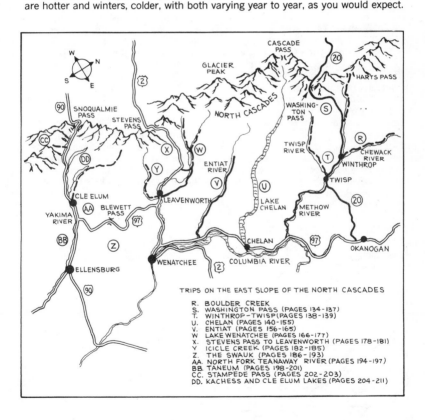

TRIPS ON THE EAST SLOPE OF THE NORTH CASCADES

R. BOULDER CREEK
S. WASHINGTON PASS (PAGES 134-137)
T. WINTHROP-TWISP (PAGES 138-139)
U. CHELAN (PAGES 140-155)
V. ENTIAT (PAGES 156-165)
W. LAKE WENATCHEE (PAGES 166-177)
X. STEVENS PASS TO LEAVENWORTH (PAGES 178-181)
Y. ICICLE CREEK (PAGES 182-185)
Z. THE SWAUK (PAGES 186-193)
AA. NORTH FORK TEANAWAY RIVER (PAGES 194-197)
BB. TANEUM (PAGES 198-201)
CC. STAMPEDE PASS (PAGES 202-203)
DD. KACHESS AND CLE ELUM LAKES (PAGES 204-211)

R BOULDER CREEK— HARTS PASS

A clear lake and crisp views—all away from the pressures of crowds. In fact, at midweek, the mountains can almost be privately yours.

Follow forest roads No. 370 and No. 391—both dusty, narrow, and high—from Winthrop through Freezeout and Lone Frank Passes to Conconully. 50 miles.

Drive 7 miles north of Winthrop on the paved road east of the Chewack River, turning east onto forest road No. 3715, and east again in less than 2 miles onto No. 370. Turn south on No. 391 at junction.

TIFFANY MOUNTAIN AND FREEZEOUT RIDGE

Farmhouses of the Okanogan valley, Glacier, and Baker from Tiffany (8242) or more modest views of the Boulder Creek drainage and the Cascades from Freezeout Ridge.

Hike 1½ miles through pine forests to reach alpine meadows on the south side of Freezeout Ridge, and first views. Add another 1½ miles and climb to the top of Tiffany for 360-degree vista sweeping from the Cascades to the hot plateaus of the Columbia Basin and eastward into the Okanogan Highlands.

Watch for trail sign at Freezeout Pass, about 4 miles north of Roger Lake Campground. Leave the trail after a ¼-mile hike in the meadows to start climb across easy grass slopes to Tiffany's top.

TIFFANY LAKE

An easy 1-mile walk to the open shores of a pretty mountain lake. Lots of places to camp and usually no other campers.

Find trail at Tiffany Springs Campground. Trail drops down from the road. Watch for mud near the lake.

CAMPGROUNDS

Note: The sites here are the formal campgrounds listed by the Forest Service. Campers, however, will find hundreds of primitive spots used in the fall by hunters.

Roger Lake—1 formal site. A poor campground near a marshy lake. 22 miles from Winthrop. Pit toilet.

Tiffany Meadows—1 formal site. A high camp at 6800 feet. 23 miles from Winthrop. Pit toilets.

Tiffany Spring—3 formal sites at the trailhead to Tiffany Lake. 25 miles from Winthrop. 22 miles from Conconully. Pit toilets. Spring water.

Salmon Meadows—13 sites. 9 miles from Conconully. Piped water. Pit toilets.

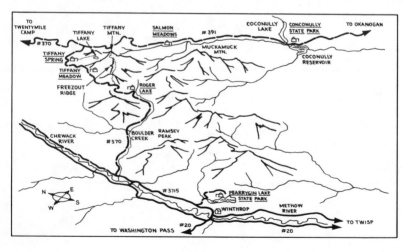

Freezeout Ridge

Conconully State Park—81 sites on
Conconully Reservoir. Restrooms.
Showers. Boat launching. Swim-
ming. Piped water. State fee.

127

Skate Peak Road

39   HARTS PASS

A winding and switchbacking forest road climbs 13 miles from Mazama to high views of the North Cascades.

Turn north off the North Cascades Highway a long mile southeast of the Early Winters Forest Service visitor information station to Mazama and then left in Mazama onto the Harts Pass road.

CASCADE CREST TRAIL

Hike out the Cascade Crest Trail either north or south of the pass for easy views of valleys, flower meadows, and peaks.

Drive south of the pass to the road end and then hike 2 miles to look into the Ninety-Nine Basin west of the crest and into Trout Creek Canyon to the east.

To follow the trail north, turn to the right at the pass, finding the trailhead on the ridge where the road switchs back on its way to the lookout. The path here winds north, over open meadows with wide vistas, toward Windy Pass and—eventually—Canada. Snow often blocks the road here through July 4.

Another short section of the trail winds south around the ridge to views out over Ninety-Nine Basin before cutting back to the east side of the crest and the end of the road (above).

On all of these trails, note how the nature of the plant life changes as you move from one side of the crest to the other. 🚶

SLATE PEAK

The lookout tower here may be burned but the vistas will remain.

Take the road north at the top of Harts Pass following it uphill past the Cascade Crest Trailhead to a gate just below the tower. Park and walk the rest of the way, giving yourself enough time to enjoy the 360-degree views from 7440 feet. It's the highest point in the state to be reached by road. The top of the mountain was flattened by the Army for a radar station.

Displays identify surrounding ridges and peaks. 🚶

SLATE MEADOW

For one of the best walks in the pass vicinity, drive up the Slate Peak road toward the lookout about ¼ mile then wander out into Slate Meadow, a broad green meadow bench.

Hike a mile or so or saunter up to the ridge top. There are some secret crystal "mines" and fossil beds in the vicinity of the ridge. Rockhounds won't tell where they are. But they're there. That's all they'll say.

CHANCELLOR-BARRON

Tumbling shacks and occasional signs of old machinery in an area which saw heavy mining activity in the 1880s and 90s.

Harts Pass Campground

Drive west from Harts Pass down a narrow road, often rough and sometimes not well-maintained, turning north on rougher spur to Barron below Windy Pass. (Road is sometimes gated, barring access to patented mining claims.) Rockhounds look for crystals and ore.

Or continue down the road to Chancellor—12 miles from the pass—for more ruins and a pleasant trails along Canyon Creek.

Cross the bridge at the end of the road, following the trail downstream as it goes along the creek toward Ross Lake. The abandoned house in the first mile once served as a stage stop and post office on a road that then ended at Barron, before the Hart Pass road was built.

CAMPGROUNDS

Gate Creek—4 sites near juncture of Gate Creek and the Methow River. 18 miles from Winthrop. Closed during 1978.

River Bend—5 sites. Turn east on road No. 3700 about 7 miles from Mazama. Campground in 1 mile. Pit toilets. Well water.

Ballard—7 sites near the Methow River. Well water. Pit toilets. 7 miles from Mazama.

Meadows—Pleasant camp at 6300 feet on spur road No. 3739, south from pass. 14 sites. In flat alpine timber area. Pit toilets. Carry water.

Chancellor—6 sites in shaded timber along Canyon Creek. 30 miles from Mazama. Pit toilets.

Harts Pass—5 sites. The original camp. No water. Pit toilets.

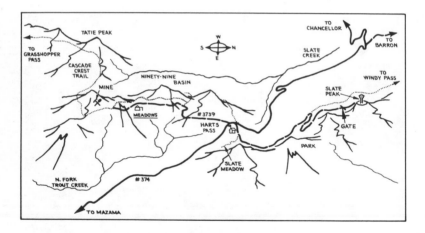

Windy Pass from Slate Peak

Sweetgrass Butte

40 NORTH CASCADES

Leave the heavily traveled North Cascades Highway for high and still higher views, walks to waterfalls and strolls through flower meadows. All north and northwest of Winthrop and Mazama.

GOAT WALL
An easy drive to spectacular views up the North Cascades Highway, down on the Methow Valley and out toward Silver Star Mountain (8901) with its glacier patches, and Gardner Mountain (8974) to the left of it.

Turn north off the North Cascade Highway nearly 2 miles south and east of the Visitor Information station at Early Winters Creek. At Mazama, just across the river, turn right (east), taking forest road No. 375, which cuts sharply back uphill to the left, in about 2 miles. In another 2.8 miles turn left again on road No. 3729.

Best views from the highway on a wide curve about 4½ miles from the Mazama road. For a hike-in view, drive another mile down the road to a cattle guard and then follow stock trails along the fence to the ridge edge in about ½ mile. Same view, almost. But more private. Snake country.

GOAT PEAK
Walk to absolutely the best views in this area from a lookout at 7000 feet.

From the Goat Wall overlook (see above) continue about 5 miles on the Goat Wall Creek road (No. 3729) to a signed spur on the right. Trailhead at the end of the spur road.

The trail starts at tree line. The first half-mile is virtually level reaching open meadows where the tread may be difficult to follow. The trail continues through open timber, climbing steeply when it climbs.

At the end: expansive views of the Methow Valley, Silver Star Mountain, the peaks of Washington Pass and the ridges of the Pasayten. †

SWEETGRASS BUTTE

Lots of blue sky and mountains in a 360-degree view from a meadow-topped mountain at 6100 feet. Camping spots off the road. But no water.

From Winthrop take the county road up the **west** side of the Chewack River. Road is north off the main highway just west of the Chewack River bridge on the outskirts of Winthrop. In about 5 miles, turn west (left) onto Cub Goat Creek Road No. 375. In another 6 miles, turn right onto Ortell Creek road No. 3600. And at Cub Pass, take the fork left uphill on road No. 3713, reaching the top of the scenic butte in about 4 more miles.

Leave time for wandering and gawking at all the Pasayten Peaks, and in spring, the flowers.

FALLS CREEK FALLS

A short walk leads to a frothy, talkative and pretty 50-foot waterfall with lots of rock ledges for viewing.

Drive north of Winthrop on the county road along the **east** side of the Chewack River (follow Pearrygin Lake signs out of town). In nearly 6 miles, turn left on paved road No. 392. Falls Creek and Falls Creek Campground in about 5.5 miles more.

Find the falls off a parking area west of the road and south of the creek. A 200-yard path loops up one side of the creek and back on the other. Pretty, even in the fall. Violent in the spring. †

CAMPGROUNDS

Memorial—2 sites near the Chewack River. Pit toilets. Well water. 7 miles north of Winthrop.

Falls Creek—7 sites in open timber near the river. 2 sites east of the road near waterfall trail. Pit toilets. Well water. 13 miles from Winthrop.

Chewack—6 sites near the river. Pit toilets. 15 miles from Winthrop.

Camp 4—4 sites in open timber on the river. Pit toilets. 18 miles from Winthrop.

Flat—9 sites in timber on Eightmile Creek. Fenced. Well water. Pit toilets. 12 miles from Winthrop on road No. 383.

Nice—3 sites that are just that off Eightmile Creek. Well water. Pit toilets. 14 miles from Winthrop on road No. 383.

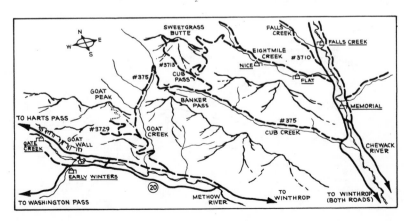

S   WASHINGTON PASS

The quiet wildness of this once remote area has most certainly been disturbed by the new North Cascades Highway. But remnants of the area's original beauty can still be found if you're willing to park your car and walk.

Drive 36.8 miles east up the North Cascades Highway from Newhalem or 35.9 miles west from Winthrop through what admittedly has to be the most magnificent "highway" scenery in the state to the highlight of the trip—Washington Pass.

A formal overlook north of the highway will give you a hint of what's to be seen here. But for greater vistas in more private settings plan to walk—not hike—over any of the several gradual trails to nearby mountain lakes.

The Forest Service has banned camping near the lakes, on nearby meadows and along highways. But enforcement of the ban has often been lax. So if you see violations, complain to rangers. And loudly. For if regulations are imposed they should apply equally to everyone.

RAINY LAKE

Sit on a log and watch waterfalls plunge off the Lyall glacier on Frisco Mountain into a clear blue lake. Beauty here is its own reward.

Find the trail at Rainy Pass—about 5 miles west from the Washington Pass complex. The very gradual path leads through pleasant forest to the small cirque lake at 4790 feet.

Less than 1 mile. The shortest walk to a lake in the area. And thus, the busiest.

LAKE ANN

A 2-mile trail leads to a pretty alpine lake in a snow-fringed cirque. Hike about 1.5 miles more and reach Maple Pass with views of Glacier Peak country to the south and the Pacific Crests to the north.

Find the trail south out of Rainy Pass. It wends its way upward to the lake and then across an open slope to the pass. Vistas much of the way. Pleasant forest the rest. With the jewel of a lake in the middle.

BLUE LAKE

Look up at the cliffs of Liberty Bell and out at Cutthroat Peak from the shores of a rock-rimmed mountain lake.

Find a new trail south of the highway just west of the Washington Pass overlook area. Trail switchbacks a very gradual 2.2 miles to the outlet of the lake. Take a sandwich and a bag of private thoughts.

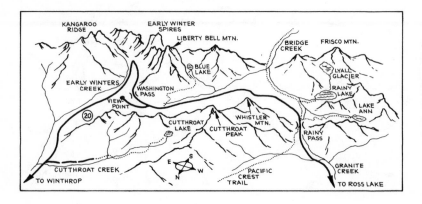

Liberty Bell (mountain) from Washington Pass

Blue Lake and Cutthroat Peak

CUTTHROAT LAKE

The signs say 2 miles but it seems only little over a mile to this lake surrounded on three sides by snow-patched peaks.

Turn uphill off the North Cascades Highway onto the Cutthroat Lake road less than 5 miles east of Washington Pass. Trail leads from a picnic area at the end of the 1-mile spur road.

Views from the trail about half-way to the lake. Either stay on the main path or take tourist trails to the left (before you cross a wooden bridge) to reach the shore, picnic spots and all sorts of views.

WASHINGTON MEADOWS

The beauty of soaring Liberty Bell and Cutthroat peaks almost—but not quite—drowns out the highway noise once you've hiked away from the road on this trail through Washington Meadows.

Walk into the meadow down any of a number of paths from the highway. An old trail makes its way leisurely through the meadows in a general westward direction reaching the highway in about 4 miles at Bridge Creek, west of the pass.

Follow established trails whenever you can. The meadows can't stand much human abuse.

Vistas here are bigger than any you'll find either from the road or the formal overlook. Snow peaks on every horizon. And fields of flowers in season, too.

CAMPGROUNDS

Early Winters—12 formal sites in a heavily used trailer-camper area off the North Cascades Highway near the Early Winters Information station and visitor center. 16 miles from Winthrop. Pit toilets. Well water. Charge camp.

Lone Fir—20 units in wooded area. 5 miles east of Washington Pass at 3600 feet. Water system. Pit toilets. Charge camp.

Klipchuck—46 units in forested area. 3 miles west of the Early Winters Information station. Flush toilets. Water system.

Fawn less than a week old

Winthrop

T   WINTHROP—TWISP

More here—at the east end of the North Cascades Highway—than the fake fronts of the redone western town of Winthrop. Take forest roads and trails nearby to lakes, lookouts and lovely views.

NORTH CASCADES SMOKEJUMPER BASE
Watch smokejumpers fold their chutes and look over their equipment at the Forest Service Smokejumping base at the Intercity Airport.

Cross the Methow River at Twisp, driving north on the county road toward Winthrop. Watch for signs indicating the airport and school in about 5 miles. Or drive south on the north side of the river from Winthrop toward Twisp.

Stop at the Visitor Information Service for an explanation of the aerial activities at the base, manned by 32 jumpers.

SHAFER MUSEUM

Pioneer furniture, tools, ancient bicycles, mining relics, sleighs, carriages, a bathtub, and even a Model T Ford.

Turn north off Highway 20, crossing the bridge into Winthrop, turning right again down the main street of the town. Watch for signs. The museum, in several old cabins, overlooks the town, the Methow River, and the mountains.

Always open on weekends and most weekdays. Hours vary, however. No admission. But donations help. 🚗

SULLIVAN'S POND

A small, but busy (bird filled) marsh just off a high-view road.

From Pearrygin Lake State Park turn east at the junction with the Winthrop road, then north in less than ¼ mile onto forest road No. 3500.

Sweeping views down on the lake and valley between the junction and the pond. At the pond, be patient. The small swamp is a world by itself. Yellow-headed blackbirds some years. And other marsh creatures too.

Road crosses part of the Winthrop Game Refuge. In fall or early spring watch for herds of deer migrating from one part of the range to the other. 🚗

LOOKOUT VIEWS (LOOKOUT MOUNTAIN)

Hike across open grass and flower meadows for vistas over Twisp and the Methow valley and out at Gardner and Midnight mountains.

Hike—uphill of course—less than 2 miles from the end of the road to a lookout at 5522 feet. Drive west at Twisp on county road 9114 and then southwest on forest road No. 3300, following the road to trailhead on spur No. 3300D.

A good hike early or late in the year. 🚶

BUTTERMILK BUTTE

Panoramic views of the Methow Valley, Twisp River and Sawtooth Ridge from the end of a road.

Drive out the Twisp River highway from downtown Twisp, turning left on road No. 3301 for 7 miles and then right for another 5 miles on a primitive but passable road. No. 3235 to a formal overlook of the area. 🚗

CAMPGROUNDS

Pearrygin Lake State Park—88 sites, most along the open shores of the lake. 5 miles from Winthrop. Restrooms. Showers. Swimming. Piped water. Popular trailer-camper area. State fee.

Blackpine Lake—34 sites on a pretty forested mountain lake with views of Hoodoo Peak. Take the river highway from Twisp, turning left on road No. 3301. In about 7 miles, turn left on road No. 3202 to the campground. Piped water. Pit toilets.

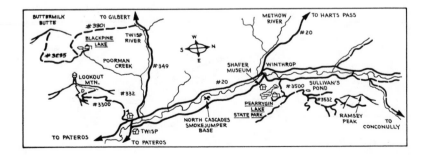

U CHELAN

An 86-mile loop drive to high ridge views of both the Chelan and Methow valleys, the Columbia River, the glacier trench of Lake Chelan, and the Cascade crest.

Turn north off Highway 150 2 miles east of Manson, turning left in ¼ mile, and right beyond Roses Lake onto the Upper Joe Creek road. Continue east past Antilon Lake to road No. 3001. (Smoothest road to the top of the ridge is from the Methow Valley on Gold Creek road No. 3107, off the highway between Methow and Carlton.)

Best views of the Lake Chelan valley from No. 3001 between the lake and the junction with No. 3002. Watch for signs of the pipeline and flume system of the Lake Chelan Reclamation District above the road.

Beyond the No. 3002 junction, the road becomes increasingly rough and narrow. Not for most passenger cars. Lake, orchard, and mountain views from South Navarre Campground, midway point on the loop.

Passing the campground, the road skirts burned-over Coyote Ridge for 10 miles, reaching views into the Methow at Saint Luise Pass-Gold Creek junction with road No. 3107 to the Methow. A rare mixture here of desert and alpine plants. Note also pumice beds alongside the road formed by material blown out of Glacier Peak.

In late July the roadside is blue with lupine between the junction and Cooper Mountain, 12.2 miles. From Cooper Mountain to Chelan, 19 miles. 🚐

COOPER MOUNTAIN VIEWPOINT

See Rainier, Stuart, the Cascades, the high peaks of the Chelan Range, the Big Bend, and the Columbia, Methow, and Lake Chelan valleys. By road from 5800 feet.

Either take the Grade Creek Loop road or drive 19 miles directly from Chelan.

Take Highway 150 west from Chelan, turning north in about 2 miles onto a paved road uphill. In another 2½ miles turn north again near an abandoned schoolhouse, turning right in another mile. Follow signs up Cooper Gulch and past Echo Valley ski area.

At the Forest Boundary sign, just north of Echo Valley, turn left. 8.1 miles to the viewpoint, mostly through heavily burned forest. A grim scene but one worth noting, nonetheless.

Viewpoint area, unburned, is a former lookout site. Camp here for supreme sunsets, night-light and dawn views. 🚐

CAMPGROUNDS

Antilon Lake—4 developed units and many undeveloped camps in a wooded area at the head of the reservoir lake located along the lake and a stream. Boating,

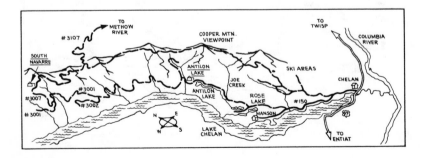

Chelan Summit from South Navarre Peak

but no motors allowed. Swimming. Lake likely to be low at the peak of the irrigation season. Occasional rattlers. Pit toilets.

South Navarre—4 units. A cool site with no mosquitoes in open pine grass and timber. Midway point on loop road. Pit toilets. Trailhead for Chelan Summit trail.

Roadside camps along the ridge-crest sections of the road overlooking Lake Chelan. Carry water. Pick the view of your choice. But remember an ax, shovel, and bucket. Fires may be banned outside formal camps in dry periods.

Lake Chelan from road No. 3001

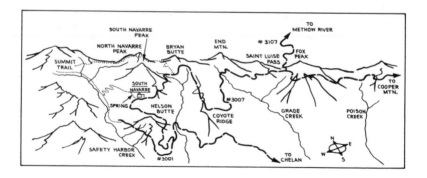

41   CHELAN SUMMIT

CHELAN SUMMIT TRAIL

A high trail leads across pine grass meadows painted with lupine and Indian paintbrush. Views to the south and the west.

Find the trail sign out of South Navarre Campground. A spring in ½ mile. Follow the trail along the mountain slope until it drops into timber in about 1 mile. Views cease here.

Trail continues on to Stehekin in 36 miles.

HIGH VIEWS

Climb over any of the open slopes between South Navarre Campground and Gold Creek junction at Saint Luise Pass for flower, mountain, and valley views.

South Navarre Peak (8000) north of the campground, and Bryan Butte (7852) offer open slopes with increasing views. Climb as high as you like.

Nelson Butte (6207), site of an abandoned lookout, about 2 miles south of South Navarre Campground, also offers views in a ¼-mile climb. An unused trail to the old lookout is often difficult to find. No building.

SUMMER BLOSSOM TRAIL

Hike to a ridge top and then pick the scenery of your choice on either side.

Drive 2½ miles north of South Navarre Campground on road No. 3001. Park in an improved spot on the right and find the hiking trail uphill to the left.

Trail climbs to the top of the ridge between the Chelan and Methow valleys and then winds north and westerly over the top of Navarre Peak. Path joins Chelan Summit trail in 5 miles.

In addition to the valleys, views here into the Glacier Peak area and the North Cascades.

Lupine

Lake Chelan and Castle Rock from Stehekin

42 LAKE CHELAN

See the entire length of the 55-mile lake in one day from Chelan to Stehekin aboard the **Lady of the Lake** from Chelan. Or stretch the trip over several days by camping along the way at any of the remote campgrounds on the lake.

A spectacular winter trip, too. Goat and deer near the shore and snow on all the hills. Gateway also to Holden and the Stehekin River valley.

CHELAN BUTTE

Sweeping views of Chelan, the green, regimented orchard country around it, the lake, the high dry plateaus of the Columbia Basin, and the broad curves of the Columbia River from an overlook point just outside the city.

Turn south (away from the lake) about 1¾ miles west of the bridge in Chelan. Watch for Chelan Butte sign. Top of the butte by gravel road in 3 miles. 3892 feet.

BEAR MOUNTAIN VIEWS

Look down on Lake Chelan and across onto the community of Manson from a high road above Lake Chelan State Park.

Turn away from the lake up the Navarre Coulee road across from the state park entrance. Turn left (east) about ½ mile beyond the switchback on the road up, following the logging road uphill at all junctions for the highest views. 13 miles. 🚐

CAMPGROUNDS

Lake Chelan State Park—201 sites. An extremely popular campground. Swimming. Boat launching. Lots of trailers. Restrooms. Showers. Piped water. State fee.

(Note: All the following campgrounds can be reached by water only, either by **Lady of the Lake** or private boat.)

Mitchell Creek—5 units. Sheltered dock. Watch for snakes. 15 miles from Chelan. Pit toilets. Lake water.

Deer Point—4 sites on a small harbor well-protected from downlake winds. Popular with small-boat owners. 22 miles from Chelan. Pit toilets. Lake water. Watch for snakes.

Safety Harbor—Undeveloped sites in an open area near the lake. 25 miles. Pit toilets. Lake water.

Big Creek—4 units and a shelter. Shaded camp on southwest side of the lake. Small falls 300 feet by trail from campground. 27 miles. Pit toilets. Lake water.

Corral Creek—2 units. 28 miles. Pit toilet. Lake water.

Graham Harbor—10 units and shelter. 31 miles. Pit toilets. Lake or creek water.

Prince Creek—5 units. On shaded bench above heavy outwash area. A newer camp. Trailhead for Lakeshore and Prince Creek trails. 35 miles. Pit toilet. Lake or creek water.

Domke Falls—3 units but room for other campers if the sites are taken. About 100 yards by trail from a spectacular falls that plunges into a pool just off the lake. 37 miles. Pit toilets. Lake water.

Refrigerator Harbor—4 units in a protected cove. Connected by a ¼-mile road to Lucerne. 41 miles. Pit toilets. Lake water.

Lucerne—2 units near guard station on a little man-made cove. Attractive camp. Good base for trips to Domke Lake and Holden. 41 miles. Pit toilets. Piped water.

Flick Creek—1 unit and shelter off lakeshore trail. 5 miles. Pit toilets. Lake water.

Moore Point—Undeveloped sites. Pit toilets.

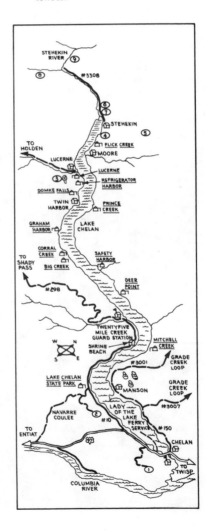

43   SLIDE RIDGE

SLIDE RIDGE VIEWS

Views down on Lake Chelan, Antilon Lake, and the towns of Manson and Chelan.

Drive about 10 miles on Slide Ridge road No. 2805 from the Ramona Park Campground. Views near the television repeater and Forest Service radio station complex. 🚙

STORMY MOUNTAIN TRAIL

One of the biggest and best views from the Devils Backbone—Glacier, Rainier, Stuart, and the crest of the Cascades.

Find trail off the Slide Ridge road No. 2805 to the left in the saddle just before the road drops down to Windy Camp. About 15 miles from Entiat-Chelan road.

Trail climbs to the ridge in about 1 mile and on to the top of Stormy Mountain in 1 more mile. An old trail continues on along the ridge to an old road above Handy Springs. Open meadows from the ridge to the top—an old lookout site. 🚶

CAMPGROUNDS

Grouse Mountain—3 sites in open timber. Isolated. Pleasant. Water from spring ½ mile down the road. Primarily a fall hunter's camp. Pit toilet.

Ramona Park—Undeveloped area. A cool camp in ponderosa pine and Douglas fir. On a spur road. Pit toilet.

Glacier lily

Lake Chelan from road No. 298

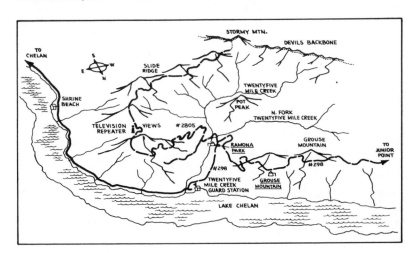

44 LUCERNE

HOLDEN

Popular entrance point to the Glacier Peak Wilderness. 12 miles by taxi from the small resort town of Lucerne on Lake Chelan. About $4 and up per person, roundtrip. Make reservations in advance with Lucerne Resort.

The Lutheran Church now operates Holden Village as a church camp under a special permit from the Forest Service. A snack bar and general store offer limited hiking supplies and equipment but no hiking food. Housing is limited to those registered in the camp programs. Emergency communication and medical facilities available.

The mining property is closed to the public. Some old mines and buildings on the south side of Railroad Creek are on private property. A visitor can, however, get a good idea of what tailing piles would look like near Image Lake if mining should ever be permitted in the wilderness.

DOMKE LAKE

A 2½-mile trail to a remote but extremely popular lake.

A good-grade trail leaves Lucerne at the boat dock—watch for signs—climbing gradually through timber to 2-site Domke Lake Camp. Resort nearby. Rent a boat and row across the lake to another small campground, Hatchery Camp, even more remote.

A Chelan air charter firm also flies campers to the lake. 🚶

LAKESHORE TRAIL

From Prince Creek Campground to Stehekin, 17.5 miles, up rock gullies, beneath steep cliffs, and along the dry steep slopes above Lake Chelan.

The **Lady of the Lake** will drop you off at any of the waypoints along the trail and pick you up at another. Make arrangements for dates and signals with the boat captain. 🚶

CAMPGROUND

Holden Campground—3 sites and other undeveloped areas along Railroad Creek just beyond the village. Views of Buckskin, Copper, Bonanza, and North Star Peaks. Pit toilets.

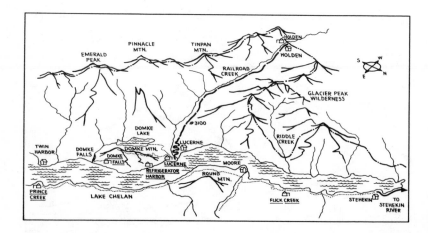

Domke Falls and Lake Chelan

Stehekin landing and McGregor Mountain

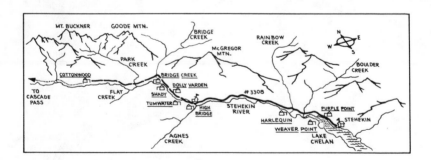

45   STEHEKIN RIVER

Hike or take a bus to a series of re-mote campsites in a beautiful valley along the park road that ends at 23 miles in the midst of North Cascades National Park.

Take the boat from Chelan to Stehekin and then catch a park bus to any of several campgrounds along a 23-mile backcountry road.

The Park operates the bus several times daily from mid-June to Labor Day as far as Cottonwood Camp with stops—wherever you want them—along the way. Fees and schedules vary from year to year.

Go up the road one day and back several days later. Or make a series of stops. Anything you wish.

Permits are required for camping or if you plan a backcountry trip. Camping is restricted to designated areas unless you camp at least a mile from any trail.

CAMPGROUNDS

Purple Point—4 sites on a pleasant, wooded slope. Road between the river and the campground. About ¼ mile from the Stehekin boat landing. Pit toilets.

Harlequin—7 units in a timbered area along the river. 5 miles from Stehekin. Popular camp with Boy Scout groups. Pit toilets.

High Bridge—3 units and a shelter on a bench about 100 feet above the river. Climb down for water. 11 miles from Stehekin. Pit toilets.

Tumwater—2 units on a ledge above the river. 13 miles from dock. Pit toilets.

Dolly Varden—1 site near the river. Pit toilet across the road. 14 miles.

Shady—1 site near the river. As the name implies, a shady spot. 15 miles. Pit toilets.

Bridge Creek—7 units and a shelter on Clear Creek. Beginning of Cascade Crest Trail to the north. Walk up the road to Bridge Creek for views of a falls. Private land nearby. 16 miles. Pit toilets.

Cottonwood—5 units at the end of the road. Trail starts here to the east side of Cascade Pass. Limited views from campground, but scenery all the way on the trail. 23 miles. Pit toilets.

Weaver Point—22 sites on Lake Chelan across the lake from the Stehekin boat dock near the mouth of the Stehekin River. Primarily a boat camp. But it can be reached by a 2-mile trail from the Harlequin Campground. Pit toilets.

Stehekin River Road

Stehekin schoolhouse

PURPLE CREEK TRAIL

Look down on Stehekin and out over Lake Chelan and the mountains at the head of the lake.

A steep trail starts a series of switchbacks toward War Creek Pass, 8 miles, near the Stehekin Post Office. High views of the lake in 1 mile through an opening in the forest.

Better views in 2 miles when trail reaches a small meadow where one can look back at Stehekin and out at the up-valley mountains.

RAINBOW FALLS

A 312-foot plume of white water plunging from a sheer cliff.

Beautiful in the summer. But in winter, a spectacle of ice-draped boulders hung with glistening icicles.

Hike up the road 4 miles from the Stehekin dock or take a park bus from the resort. A tour bus also makes the trip to the falls and back during the stopover of the boat from Chelan.

SCHOOLHOUSE

The only one-teacher log school still operating in the state. The building was constructed in 1921 of trees harvested from nearby forest land by local people who contributed their time to build the school. The building occupies National Forest land under a special-use permit. ½ mile downriver from the falls alongside the main road.

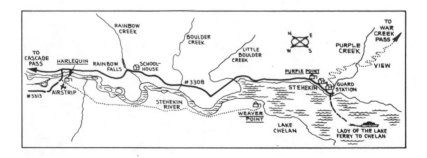

Rainbow Falls

46   AGNES GORGE

A walk through high and dry forest leads to up-valley views of peaks in the Glacier Peak Wilderness.

Find the trail uphill beyond High Bridge and beyond the Cascade Crest Trail about a quarter-mile, to the left. The path starts out in forest with no views anywhere until it reaches the wilderness boundary in about 1 mile.

From then on the trail winds above the Agnes Creek Gorge with almost constant vistas ahead until it ends in pleasant forest at small waterfalls. Come back the same way. 🚶

COON LAKE

A 1-mile hike with occasional down-valley views to a boggy lake.

Take the McGregor Mountain trail near the High Bridge Guard Station. On the north side of the road. Trail climbs through timber to a rocky point near the lake for views down the Stehekin River valley.

A polliwog lake, high in spring, low in summer. 🚶

BASIN CREEK

An easy 2-mile walk leads to higher and higher vistas of ridges, peaks and waterfalls on the east side of scenic Cascade Pass.

Take the trail out of Cottonwood Camp at the end of the road from Stehekin. Views increase as the trail steadily makes its way up the valley toward the pass, in 8 miles.

A spectacular short walk. Waterfalls at Basin Creek. 🚶

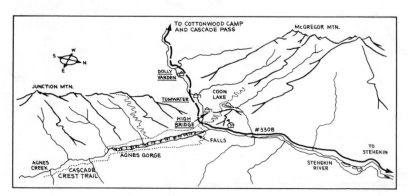

High Bridge on Stehekin River

Lincoln Rock

V   ENTIAT

ROCKY REACH DAM
Fish-viewing rooms, motion pictures, murals, Indian history, and industrial exhibits.

Drive north 7 miles from Wenatchee on Highway 97. Watch for signs to parking area on the right.

Windows in the side of the fish ladder that climbs from the river to the top of the dam permit underwater views of migrating salmon, steelhead, and trout in a viewing gallery in the Visitor Center.

An Indian exhibit on early history of the Columbia Basin, an industrial display prepared by commercial power purchasers, and a topographic map of the state are features of a powerhouse display. Films on construction of the dam and about the Chelan-Wenatchee area are shown almost continuously in the Visitor Center Auditorium.

Self-guided tours include views of the dam, generators, murals, and occasional summertime art shows. 🚗

LINCOLN ROCK
Lincoln's profile in the side of a mountain overlooking the Columbia River behind Rocky Reach Dam.

Drive north of the dam on Highway 97 a little more than 1 mile, turning uphill at the Swakane Canyon road No. 252. Stop and look up at the cliffs. 🚗

ENTIAT RIDGE

Airplane views of the Columbia, Lake Wenatchee, Glacier, Stuart, and the Cascades.

A high, sometimes steep and skittish road along the top of Entiat Ridge from Chumstick past Sugarloaf to Maverick Saddle. The airborne, squeamish sections are very real but short, thankfully, and safe. Road generally open late in June when country is at its best.

To start with high views of the Columbia, turn south off the Entiat River road up the Entiat Summit road No. 2924 at Mills Canyon about 3¼ miles east of Entiat. First high views in about 10 miles. Chumstick—an abandoned lookout site—in 17 miles. French Corral, a road intersection point, in 27 miles.

To start with views of Lake Wenatchee and mountains to the west, turn south off the Entiat River road at Ardenvoir onto Mad River road No. 119A, turning left in a little more than 2 miles onto No. 2615. Watch signs carefully. French Corral Junction in 13 miles.

Best views in the first several miles from French Corral north. Road ducks into timber at about Sugarloaf Corral.

To drop down into the Lake Wenatchee area, take road No. 2722 west out of Maverick Saddle, dropping 6 miles to the Chiwawa River road. 🚐

SUGARLOAF LOOKOUT

Expansive views of the Stuart Range, Stuart, Glacier, Snowgrass, Rainier's tip, Cashmere, the brown plains of the Columbia Basin, and the stark ridges of the Chelan-Okanogan mountains.

5 miles from French Corral. Watch for sign. ¼-mile spur road leads past primitive camping area to lookout building perched atop an irregular group of basalt columns. Several other shafts of basalt stand alone on the slopes of the mountain. 🚐

Note: Over 65,000 acres of forest were swept by lightning-caused fires in August, 1970. Rehabilitation work continues. For views of the breadth of the destruction in this area visit Sugarloaf Lookout (above), Tyee Mountain Lookout, Big Hill and Junior Point.

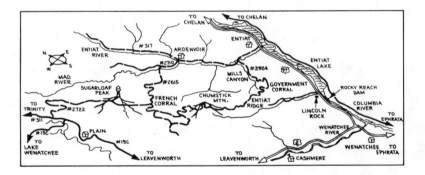

Forest road No. 2900

47   ENTIAT RIVER

From hot, dry valleys to cool alpine meadows with waterfalls, river trails, and viewpoints in between.

From Entiat, 40 miles to end of the road and the head of the Entiat River trail, leading to Myrtle Lake in 4 miles and Entiat Meadows in 15.

High roads generally open in late June.

CAMPGROUNDS

Pine Flats—9 units, designed for tents and small trailers in open ponderosa pine forest near the Mad River. 4 units near the river, the rest away. An ideal spring and late-fall camp. Hot in summer. Pit toilets. 11 miles from Entiat.

Fox Creek—8 units on a tree-shaded flat next to the Entiat River. All units, however, are back from the river. The first campground to fill up on weekends. 27 miles from Entiat. Pit toilets.

Lake Creek—12 units located on a bench above the river. One unit on Lake Creek. 28 miles from Entiat. Pit toilets.

Silver Falls—44 units in two campground areas on either side of Silver Creek. First—downriver—site in large, shady timber with about half the sites near the river. Upriver campground on one timbered loop with sites well separated. Wells. Pit toilets.

North Fork—8 units about 25 yards off the highway. Tends to be dusty in summer. Near river. 33 miles from Entiat. Pit toilets.

Spruce Grove—2 units next to the river in well-worn, heavily used area under big timber. Often crowded on weekends. 35 miles from Entiat. Pit toilets.

Three Creek—3 units about 50 yards from the river in lodgepole pine. On spur road off main Entiat valley road 36 miles from Entiat. Pit toilets.

Cottonwood—26 units, most oriented to the river. A few off the main road, tending to be dusty. Most across the bridge on a loop downriver. 38 miles from Entiat. Wells. Pit toilets.

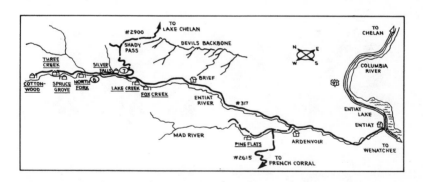

48   MAD RIVER

TYEE MOUNTAIN LOOKOUT

Sweeping vistas here, once, of timbered mountains and snow-topped peaks. Now look out at the horrible and overwhelming destruction wrought by forest fires.

Not necessarily a beautiful trip. But one still worth taking if only to appreciate the violence of fire.

Turn toward the river at Ardenvoir onto Mad River road No. 119A keeping right at the Pine Flat Campground junction onto road No. 2809. Road to the lookout gets increasingly rough toward the end. Tower at 6680 feet.

From Ardenvoir to lookout, 21 miles.

MAD RIVER TRAIL

An easy and pleasant hike through a shady river canyon from the Pine Flat Campground.

Find trail off the turnaround in the campground. Trail follows the river to Hornet Creek and beyond. Touched only slightly by fire. Most pleasant in the first mile. And watch for a small grove of trees that a beaver once envisioned using for his dam. The beaver's efforts still show even though the trees still live.

Note also how some of the older Douglas fir and cedar trees survived the blistering ground fires that crossed the trail in places.

YOUNG CREEK SHELTER

A 2-mile hike along the Mad River to a shelter in a small open meadow.

Turn south (left) off the road to Tyee Lookout road No. 2809 onto road No. 279. Drive to Camp 9—a primitive hunter's camp—at the end of the road.

Spur trail leads westerly from camp down to the Mad River trail, following the river upstream to the shelter near Young Creek.

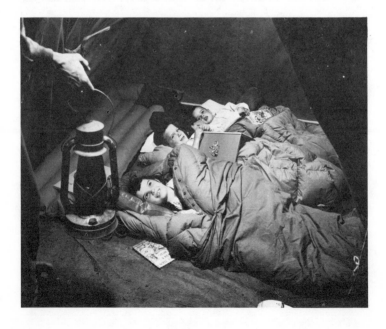

Mad River Trail

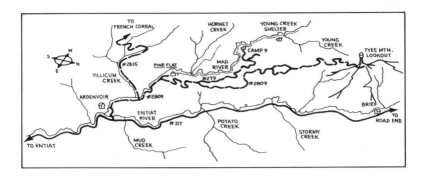

Silver Falls

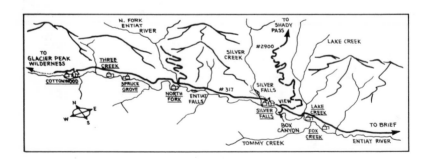

Silver Falls Trail

49   SILVER FALLS

A lace-like veil of water hanging from a 50-foot cliff.

By nature trail from the Silver Falls Campground. ¼ mile. Find sign on uphill side of the road across from the upper campground entrance.

Trail climbs a series of switchbacks with stone steps in steepest pitches and occasional places to rest. Views of the falls from the upper end of the trail. Or hike to the top and cool off behind the curtain of water.

BOX CANYON OVERLOOK

A 75-foot-deep narrow gorge gouged through solid rock, roaring its loudest in the spring.

Watch for sign about 2 miles downriver from the Silver Falls Campground. Follow a short spur road toward the river to a parking area, walking directly toward the river to a formal overlook area.

Fence protects a path over rock slabs for views into the canyon.

ENTIAT FALLS

A stubby torrent plunges through a rock cleft. A cool place to rest.

Watch for sign about 3 miles upriver from the Silver Falls Campground. Find the waterfall just past the parking area.

Water ouzels (dippers) some years nest in corners of rock overhangs below the falls. Look for yellow mouths gaping from small nest holes in moss.

VALLEY VIEW

One of the very few views up the forested Entiat valley from the valley floor.

Watch for marked vista point on the south side of the road at the Shady Pass road junction, 1 mile downriver from Silver Falls Campground.

Profile sign identifies Maude, Gopher, Saska, and Duncan Hill.

Entiat burn near Shady Pass

50   ENTIAT VALLEY TO LAKE CHELAN

High views off a narrow, sometimes steep, and often dusty forest road. Much of this area was burned over in the forest fires of 1970.

From the Entiat River near the Lake Creek Forest Camp over the Chelan Mountain at Shady Pass to Lake Chelan near the Twentyfive Mile Creek Guard Station. About 24 miles.

Shady Pass

BIG HILL VIEW

Drive 2 miles from Shady Pass along a narrow road through timber to long views of Lake Chelan, Glacier, and Rainier and closer looks at the devastating effects of a wild forest fire.

A cool 6800 feet on a hot summer day.

Walk past the cabin shelter at the end of the road to the one-time site of a lookout tower. But for bigger views prowl open nearby meadows.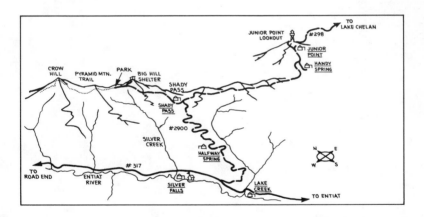

JUNIOR POINT

Glacier, the top of Rainier, the Navarre Peaks, and the scorched mountains of the Okanogans from a viewpoint (6676) atop an alpine knoll.

Watch for Junior Point signs about 12 miles from Lake Chelan. Viewpoint about 100 yards beyond the Junior Point Campground.

CAMPGROUNDS

Halfway Spring—5 units. A pleasant camp at mid-elevation in open timber. All sites except one back away from the road. Pit toilets.

Shady Pass—1 unit at the junction of the Big Hill road at the top of the pass. A pleasant shaded semi-alpine site. Water from a spring downhill to the west of the camp. Pit toilet.

Big Hill—A garage converted into a shelter with expansive views. Condition of the shelter is as good as the last visitor left it. Pit toilet. Haul water from Shady Pass.

Handy Spring—1 unit at the end of a short spur road. A primitive unkempt site in a sometimes muddy area. Piped spring water. Pit toilet.

Junior Point—5 sites in a cool alpine (6600) setting near viewpoint. Off the main road. Surrounded by lupine slopes and subalpine timber. Water in camp from cistern in summer. Pit toilets.

W LAKE WENATCHEE

Three valley recreation areas linked to the hub of a big lake.

Roads up the Little Wenatchee, White, and Chiwawa River valleys lead away from the heavy camping pressures on the lake to trails, falls, old mining towns, and high views.

Unpaved river roads are likely to be dusty or muddy, depending on the weather. But the river campgrounds, in many instances, offer some of the better camping opportunities in the area.

Note: Only campgrounds of more than 2 sites are listed here. Smaller camps can be found along valley roads, particularly up the Chiwawa River.

LAKE WENATCHEE CAMPGROUNDS

Lake Wenatchee State Park—197 sites on timber loops, mostly away from the lake. An extremely heavily used area. Swimming. Boating. Saturday evening movies. Restrooms. Showers. Piped water. State fee.

Nason Creek—75 sites on both sides of the road to the state park. Often mistaken for the state park. Popular trailer area. Group trailer loop. Piped water. Pit toilets. Federal fee.

Twin Lakes

Glacier View—23 sites. An extremely pleasant tent-only campground at the far end of the South Shore Lake Wenatchee road. Walk-in sites from parking spurs on campground loop. Some sites on lake. No trailers. Pit toilets. Federal fee.

LITTLE WENATCHEE RIVER CAMPGROUNDS

Riverside—6 units near Little Wenatchee River on spur off Rainy Creek road. All sites near the river in large timber area. 8 miles from Lake Wenatchee. Pit toilets.

Soda Springs—5 sites near a soda spring. Units on both sides of campground spur road. 8 miles west of Lake Wenatchee. Mosquitoes, usually. Pit toilets. No trailers.

Lake Creek—8 sites in open timber area away from the road. A pleasant campground even though sites are not well-defined. 13 miles from Lake Wenatchee. Pit toilets.

Little Wenatchee Ford—3 sites in open area at the end of the road. Modest views. Busy despite lack of development. 18 miles from Lake Wenatchee. Pit toilets. No trailers.

WHITE RIVER CAMPGROUNDS

Napeequa—5 sites near Napeequa River bridge. Pit toilets.

Grasshopper Meadows—5 sites on the west side of the road in wooded site. Meadow across the road.

Raccoon

Short hike to the river. 8 miles from Lake Wenatchee. Pit toilets.

White River Falls—5 units along the White River. Waterfall attracts heavy vehicle traffic through camp. 9 miles from Lake Wenatchee. Pit toilets. No trailers.

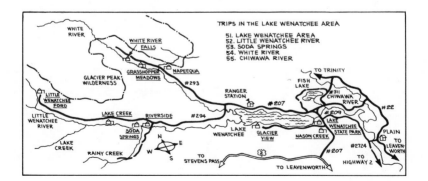

167

51   LAKE WENATCHEE AREA

HIDDEN LAKE
A steep ½-mile walk leads to a pretty boulder-bound mountain lake about 500 feet above Lake Wenatchee.

Find trail off lake shore at upper (west) end of Glacier View Campground. In parking area. Watch for sign. Trail crosses bridge then wends through timber to popular lake.

Paths around the boulder-strewn shore. Lots of places to picnic, contemplate or just plain snooze. 🚶

SOUTH SHORE LAKE TRAIL
An easy level trail leads out of Glacier View Campground about 1 ½ miles to a Campfire Girl camp to the east.

Pick up trail in the campground between tent sites and the lake, following it eastward past summer homes to the formal camp. Trail follows lake shore all the way. 🚶

TWIN LAKES
Walk an easy ½-mile up a crummy trail after driving 10 miles through clear cuts for pleasant view of mountains over a pretty lake.

Take the Chiwawa road No. 311 past Fish Lake turning northerly at junction of Meadow Creek road 2815. Trail, at the end of the road in 10 miles, climbs up an old cat track and then winds downhill to deadend at the lake. View of the snow-covered peaks above the Napeequa Valley. 🚶

GLACIER PEAK VIEWS
Glacier (10,568) framed up the White River valley between David (7431) and the White Mountains.

Drive west past the Lake Wenatchee Ranger Station about 2 miles, turning south on the Little Wenatchee River road No. 283. Viewpoint, marked with signs, at the bridge over the White River. 🚗

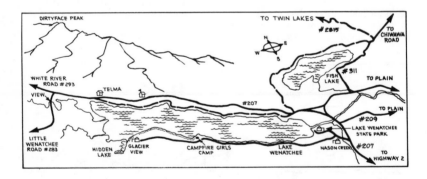

Hidden Lake

Porcupine

52 LITTLE WENATCHEE RIVER

BLACKBERRIES AND VIEWS

Blackberry thickets in clear cuts with high views of Lake Wenatchee, Nason Ridge, and the Little Wenatchee River valley.

Turn north on Line Creek road No. 2711—the first road west of Lake Wenatchee off the Little Wenatchee River road—keeping right at the first turn. Formal viewpoint in 3 miles. Best blackberries in logged-over areas on the way.

For views and berries along Soda Springs road No. 2718, turn north from the Little Wenatchee road just beyond the buildings of the abandoned Ideal Cement Company's limestone quarry—now Girl Scout property. Keep left at the first junction. Add Labyrinth (6360) to the view. 🚙

LITTLE WENATCHEE TRAIL

A 1½-mile trail along a pretty canyon on the sparkling Little Wenatchee River. Rocks, bluffs, tumbling rapids, and deep pools.

Trail leaves the back, southwest corner, of the Lake Creek Campground. Find sign. The trail climbs a ridge above the river before dropping down to pass a series of riffles and rapids, climbing again along the rim of the canyon near the end of the trail. Whenever the trail leaves the river, watch for spur paths leading to loops along the gorge. An extremely pleasant walk. 🚶

Lake Wenatchee from Line Creek Road

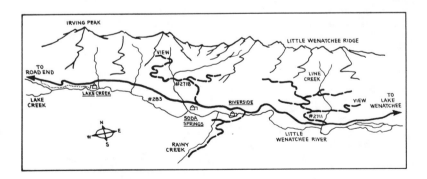

53   SODA SPRINGS

Soda-pop spring, a rock to carve on, and trails through forests and to viewpoints.

Find the soda spring and the soft soapstone boulder to the left of the entrance road into Soda Springs Campground.

Dip soda water—bring your own flavoring, nature supplies the fizzin'—from a boxed spring about 20 feet from a parking area.

Find the initial rock up a short trail beyond the spring, turning right at the first fork.

And it's perfectly all right to carve here. In fact, the Forest Service encourages it—hoping to save a few tables and signs in the process.

BLUFF VIEW TRAIL

A modest view of an old limestone quarry and the Little Wenatchee River valley.

Turn left at the junction to Initial Rock, following tourist trails and old switchbacks constantly uphill to a former lookout site. ¼ mile. Trail downhill is just as confusing. Note turning points on the way up.

BIG TREE LOOP TRAIL

A pleasant ½-mile loop trail through a creek-bottom stand of cedar. The "big" trees aren't the big trees of the Puget Sound region, but rather excellent examples of bigger timber found on the dry side of the Cascades.

Find trail at the far end of the Soda Springs Campground, bearing to the right. Watch for signs. Trail drops across a small creek to the Little Wenatchee River.

MINE VIEW TRAIL

A short trail to a bluff overlooking the Little Wenatchee River and glimpses through the trees of the limestone quarry to the east.

Find trail at the end of the campground road into Soda Springs Campground. From the river overlook point, follow trail to the left for view of quarry. Trail eventually drops down to rich cedar forest area along the river. To viewpoints, less than ¼ mile.

LITTLE WENATCHEE FALLS

A pretty series of stubby torrents through huge boulders with crystal pools. At the lower end, massive snarls of logs.

Find unmarked way-trail off the paved Little Wenatchee River road about 50 yards east of the junction with Rainy Creek road No. 2728. The narrow trail, beyond rocks piled off the road, drops steeply but quickly to a faded Wenatchee Falls sign.

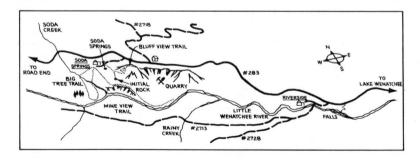

Little Wenatchee River Falls

Rock slabs above the noisy river afford ideal lunch spots. Note bowls being eroded into the tops of some slabs. Small pebbles and stones, often still inside the dishes, grind the bowls larger in the swirling action of high water.

For a bigger spectacle, visit the falls in the spring.

173

Lake Wenatchee from Dirtyface Viewpoint

54   WHITE RIVER

Viewpoints, history sites, waterfalls, and forest trails along a formal tour route. Watch for signs.

WHITE RIVER VIEWS
The "Poet Peaks" of Little Wenatchee Ridge—from the left, Irving, Poe, Longfellow, Whittier, and Bryant—and including Lake Wenatchee, Nason Ridge, and on the way down, Glacier.

Turn east off the White River road about 2½ miles from the intersection with the Little Wenatchee River road. Watch for Dirty Face logging road sign. Drive 2.3 miles to a marked viewpoint.

WHITE RIVER FALLS
The White River plunges over rock slabs into a narrow canyon.

Walk out over rock outcrops from the White River Falls Campground to views down over the water chute. No fence protects the area and rocks can be extremely slippery when wet.

A way-trail leads around to the left through boulders to the bottom of the canyon and limited views of the falls. Best views across the river. See Panther Creek Trail.

PANTHER CREEK TRAIL
A pleasant 1-mile walk back along the west side of the White River leads to full-face views of White River Falls.

Drive to the end of the White River road, taking trail to the left across the footbridge. A spur trail forks left to the falls in a little less than a mile.

A narrow way-trail leads uphill from the first falls viewpoint to a second overlook with a fuller view.

GLACIER PEAK WILDERNESS TRAILS
Two trails on either side of the White River lead to the boundary of the Glacier Peak Wilderness in about 2 miles.

Both lead through pleasant timber, sometimes near the river, sometimes not. The two trails—the White River on the east bank and the Indian Creek on the west—are not connected at the wilderness boundary.

HISTORY SITE
A concrete cross on the west side of the White River road, 2 miles from the Little Wenatchee road junction, marks the grave of Eunice Henry, a homesteader who died here in 1913. Remnants of her cabin and overgrown sections of the old wagon road to the east of the road on a short loop trail. See sign.

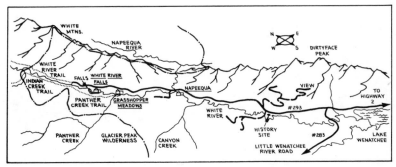

55   CHIWAWA RIVER

TRINITY

Buildings and old mill of the defunct Royal Development Mine at the end of the Chiwawa River road.

Trail to the Glacier Peak Wilderness leads across bridge, gated to vehicle traffic, through the center of the private town. All the buildings are posted and probably dangerous. Don't explore off the trail without permission of the caretaker.

PHELPS CREEK ROAD

High views of the icefields on Buck Mountain, Chiwawa Ridge, and the Chiwawa River valley.

Turn east on the first road (No. 3000) south of the Phelps Creek Campground. Best views in about 2½ miles at about 3000 feet.

Road is rough but passable to passenger cars. 🚙

HALFWAY HOUSE

An abandoned two-story log cabin on open meadows of an old homestead tract which once served as a halfway resting point for travelers bound for Trinity.

Watch for the cabin on the far side of meadows to the east of the road just north of Chikamin Creek, less than 1¼ miles north of Grouse Creek Campground.

Cabin and the meadows are privately owned.

CAMPGROUNDS

Goose Creek—4 units in wooded area next to Goose Creek. On lower Chiwawa road No. 2746. Pit toilet.

Deep Creek—3 units at junction of Deep Creek and Lower Chiwawa roads. Pit toilet.

Deer Camp—3 units in high view site off main switchback on road No. 2722. No water. Pit toilet.

Grouse Creek—4 units in wooded area near Grouse Creek. 26 miles from Leavenworth. Pit toilets.

Rock Creek—4 units near road. Likely to be very dusty. Piped water. Pit toilets. 29 miles from Leavenworth.

Rock Creek Crossing—4 units in sparsely wooded area near Rock Creek. Pit toilets. 31 miles from Leavenworth.

Schaefer Creek—3 sites on Chiwawa River in timber. Pit toilets. 33 miles from Leavenworth.

Atkinson Flat—4 formal sites near the Chiwawa River in a huge meadow. Pit toilets.

19 mile—3 units above the river on a steep bank in a wooded area. Pit toilets.

Maple Creek—7 sites across the Chiwawa River on a spur road. Watch for sign. Sites away from the river in shady timber. 37 miles from Leavenworth. Pit toilets.

Alpine Meadow—4 units in pleasant open meadow near river. Pickup and tent campers only. 38 miles from Leavenworth. Pit toilets.

Phelps Creek—7 units on a very pleasant shady spur along the Chiwawa River just below the end of the road at Trinity. 39 miles from Leavenworth. Pit toilets.

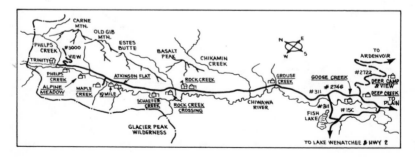

Trinity Mine buildings below Buck Mountain

Morning mist near Leavenworth

X   STEVENS PASS TO LEAVENWORTH

From the alpine slopes of Stevens Pass to the remodeled Bavarian-style town of Leavenworth.

A spectacular drive for color-seekers in the fall with spur roads and trails leading to higher views, lakes, and quiet river drives.

LAKE SUSAN JANE TRAIL

A pretty subalpine lake on the Cascade Crest Trail. ¾ mile from the end of the Mill Creek road No. 2617—if you can drive that far. Turn south off Highway 2 about 6 miles from Stevens Pass. Road gets increasingly steeper and rougher as it nears the top, not designed for passenger cars. A powerline access road.

Drive as far as you can, hiking on up the road to the Cascade Crest Trail, turning left. Josephine Lake, headwater of Icicle Creek, another 1½ miles. ↑

LANHAM LAKE

An easy 1.8 mile walk just off the Stevens Pass Highway to a pleasant mountain lake at 3900 feet.

Find the trail to the east of road No. 2617 just beyond Lanham Creek. Park in a clear area on the right. Trail starts in timber then breaks out into an ugly powerline right-of-way. Make your way generally uphill by walking first to the right and then left on roads, watching for an old logging track or blazes on trees.

Trail follows an old logging spur before entering timber again, ending at a very pleasant picnic or camp spot on the lake.

Turn south off Highway 2 about 6 miles from Stevens Pass (see Lake Susan Jane) finding trail head in less than ¼ mile. ↑

NASON RIDGE TRAIL

Hike 1½ miles through open timber to high views from the east end of Nason Ridge in a saddle below Round Mountain. Look out on Stevens Pass Highway, the Chiwaukum Range and down on Lake Wenatchee.

Turn north off Highway 2 onto Butcher Creek road No. 2717 (no sign) about .2 mile east of the state highway rest stop. Forest road crosses a cleared area and bridge in ½ mile. Follow signs to trail head, on the right in 4.7 miles.

Water at Spring Camp on trail about ½ mile from the road. Best views on the ridge 100 yards right or left from trail junction through trees on the north side of the ridge. ↑

CAMPGROUNDS

White Pine—6 sites just off Highway 2 on White Pine Creek road No. 266. Turn south off Highway 2 about 1 mile west of Merritt. Pit toilets.

Tumwater—56 camping and 27 picnic units in a wooded area between Chiwaukum Creek and the Wenatchee River. A popular, heavily used campground. 9 miles northwest of Leavenworth on Highway 2. Piped water. Toilets. Federal fee.

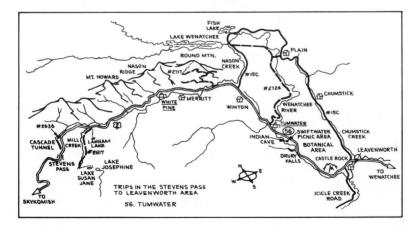

56. TUMWATER

Lewisia tweedyi

56   TUMWATER

WENATCHEE RIVER ROAD
A quiet, beautiful section of the Wenatchee River away from the hubbub of highways. Riffles and rapids under bald cliffs between the community of Plain and Tumwater Canyon.

Turn right (east) onto the first forest road (No. 2724), just north of the Tumwater Campground and the Chiwaukum Creek bridge. Sign says road not maintained by county.

The road wanders 3¾ miles along the river before climbing along a cliff-like ridge to a paved road leading to Plain, 9.3 miles.

The lower road is likely to be dusty in summer and muddy in spring. The narrow, undeveloped ridge road section—1¼ miles—can be extremely hazardous after a rain. Dust turns into slime.

From Plain either return via Lake Wenatchee or through Chumstick to Leavenworth. Follow signs.

DRURY FALLS
Spring torrents pour off the cliffs of Icicle Ridge into the Wenatchee River Canyon.

1 mile downriver from the Swiftwater Picnic Area. Watch for falls on cliffs across the river.

CASTLE ROCK
A favorite practice area for rock climbers with airy views from the top of the Tumwater Canyon.

Indian cave

Drive 3 miles west of Leavenworth on Highway 2. Parking area at the base.
An unmarked scramble-route up grass and scree slopes leads to similar views
without the necessity of rock climbing.

INDIAN CAVE

Nature trail from the Swiftwater Picnic Area leads to an Indian "cave" under
the crest of a huge boulder on the Wenatchee River.

Drive 8 miles north of Leavenworth. Short trail up-river from the upper picnic
area leads to the cave. Signs of smoke on the ceiling of the rock shelter establish
setting for Indian fishermen waiting out a storm.

LEWISIA TWEEDYI

The rarest of three species of Lewisia.

Preserved in a two-square-mile botanical preserve about 5 miles north of
Leavenworth but sometimes seen along the highway near the Swiftwater Picnic
Area. Look for yellow or salmon-colored blooms in May and June. But don't pick.
They are extremely rare. Take a picture, leaving the blossom for others to enjoy
too.

Y   ICICLE CREEK

Clear, deep pools and chattering rapids on a creek as crisply beautiful as its name.

Turn south off Highway 2 at sign just west of Leavenworth. Road remains near the creek most of the way up the valley.

Catch glimpses of Stuart up the Eightmile Creek valley at the top of the hill just beyond the Eightmile Campground.

Coolest camping at Johnny Creek and above. Some rattlesnakes below Johnny Creek.

BOUNDARY BUTTE VIEWPOINT

From 3168 feet, look down on the orchards of Leavenworth and Cashmere, out into the Enchantment Lake peaks and the Icicle Creek drainage and up to Glacier Peak. With wildflowers in the spring.

Cross the bridge over the Wenatchee River just east of the Leavenworth Ranger Station in Leavenworth, taking the first road right off the highway. In 100 yards

Cashmere Peak from Johnny Creek Road

turn left on the Mountain Home road No. 2415. Follow signs. Road views down on Leavenworth in the first mile.

In 6 miles turn east onto the lookout spur road. Old lookout site in 2 more miles. Road No. 2415 continues southeast to the Blewett Pass highway. 🚐

LEAVENWORTH NATIONAL FISH HATCHERY
Largest federal fish hatchery in the United States.

Built in 1939 after Grand Coulee Dam blocked upstream migration of salmon. Over 8 million coho and chinook salmon are hatched here each year.

Turn south onto the Icicle Creek road at the west end of Leavenworth. About 1½ miles south of the Wenatchee River bridge. Watch for signs. 🚐

JOHNNY CREEK ROAD
Views of Cashmere Peak (8520), the Icicle valley, 6600 Ridge, and Bootjack (6700).

Turn north off the Icicle Creek road about 400 feet east of the Johnny Creek Campground, keeping right at the first forest road intersection. Views from road No. 2436 in less than 2 miles. 🚐

EIGHTMILE LAKE
Hike past a small lake to a much larger one tucked in timber below towering rock walls.

Turn south off the Icicle River road at Bridge Creek Campground onto road No. 2412. Trail is well-signed about 3 miles up the road. Valley views enroute.

The trail climbs sharply, to start with, straight up the ridge to (of all things) the end of a logging road. (Some hikers take the road down, others drive up it as far as they can get. Turn uphill on the first road spur below the trail parking area.)

From the end of the logging road, the trail quickly becomes a pleasant forest path reaching Little Eightmile Lake (4400) in 2½ miles and then, after a quick climb through a rock slide, Eightmile Lake itself (4641) in another half-mile.

The first part of the trail was "skyline" logged in 1972, assertedly to protect recreation values. Judge for yourself. 🚶

CAMPGROUNDS
Eightmile—9 sites on two loops between the road and creek. All sites less than 100 feet from the Icicle. Many closer. 8 miles from Leavenworth. Pit toilets.

Bridge Creek—8 units. Sites oriented to creek. 9 miles from Leavenworth. Pit toilets.

Johnny Creek—16 units. First of the cooler campgrounds. Sites off two spurs. Some away from the creek but most near it. Piped water. Pit toilets. 12 miles from Leavenworth.

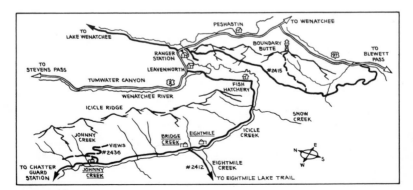

Icicle Creek at Chatter Creek Guard Station

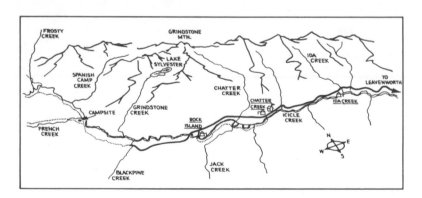

57   UPPER ICICLE CREEK

ICICLE CREEK BRIDAL TRAIL

A water-grade walk past pools, big rocks and more pools between the Chatter Guard Station and Rock Island Campground. 2 easy miles.

Cross Icicle Creek on footbridge at the guard station, walking upstream on trail along the river. Or find the trail across the bridge from the Rock Island Campground and walk downstream. High water in Trout and Jack Creeks during the spring may block the way. Worth the walk, though, anytime.

FRENCH CREEK CAMP

An easy 1½-mile walk through timber down the Icicle Creek trail to a noisy rapids and a pleasant camping spot. A good place for a test-run backpacking trip.

Drive across Icicle Creek at Rock Island Campground, following the Blackpine road to the end. Trail, at the end of the road, winds up the valley but away from the river until it reaches the camp.

Find the rapids—you'll hear them hustling—off to the right of the trail before it crosses the bridge.

CAMPGROUNDS

Ida Creek—6 units in timbered area near creek which has slowed down here to riffles over gravel. Sites between road and creek. 15 miles from Leavenworth. Pit toilets.

Chatter Creek—12 units away from the Icicle on two small forks of Chatter Creek. 3 walk-in sites reached by log bridge in the middle of the campground. Pleasant shaded area. 17 miles from Leavenworth. Pit toilets.

Rock Island—21 units in four camping areas. Three groups of sites off spurs above and below the bridge. One small camping area across the bridge. All are signed. 19 miles from Leavenworth. Pit toilets.

Yellow violets

Arrastra, an ore grindstone, at Blewett townsite

Z   THE SWAUK

Highway 97 from Cle Elum to Wenatchee races up this valley but viewfinders and campers get off the main highway and into the surrounding hills. Mines once were the biggest attraction in the valley. Some prospectors still try for fortunes. Campers, however, will look for agates, views, and fossils.

Drive east from Seattle on I-90, turning off at Wenatchee Interchange No. 85, east of Cle Elum. Continue east on highway 97. Liberty Guard Station 13 miles from the junction. Swauk Pass in another 11 miles.

CAMPGROUNDS

Mineral Springs—11 sites at the junction of Medicine and Swauk Creeks. A wooded area just off the highway. 3 miles north of Liberty Guard Station. Some sites oriented to the creek. Pit toilets. Spring water.

Swauk—22 sites in wooded loops below the highway on Swauk Creek. Some sites near the stream, others in shady timbers. 3000 feet elevation. Piped water. Restrooms and pit toilets. 7 miles from guard station. Charge.

Tronsen—23 sites in heavy timber. Most sites on Tronsen Creek. Some near a meadow at the upper end of the campground. 1 mile north of Swauk Pass. Pit toilets.

Bonanza—5 sites in a small camp squeezed in open timber between the highway and Tronsen Creek. Pit toilets. Well.

Park—3 sites in wooded area along old Blewett Pass Highway. Pit toilets. Less than 1 mile north of Highway 97.

Lion Rock Spring—3 sites in a patch of timber near a fenced spring below Lion Rock. Horse corral. Pit toilets. Spring. 8 miles from Swauk Pass.

Undeveloped camp spots are to be found in most of the high areas on both sides of the highway. Pick your own but carry ax, bucket, shovel, and water.

Mount Rainier from road No. 2100

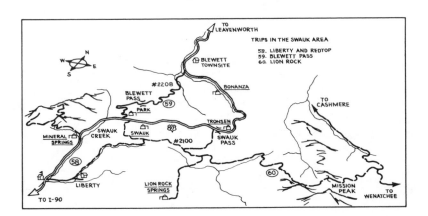

58   LIBERTY AND RED TOP

A cross-section view here of man's relationship to mineral.

Leave I-90 at the Wenatchee Interchange east of Cle Elum, driving north toward Wenatchee on Highway 97. Liberty Guard Station in 13 miles.

LIBERTY

If you've ever wondered what a mining dredge can do to a pretty creek take a long look at the private gold-dredging operation on Williams Creek in the old mining town of Liberty.

Turn east off Highway 97 at the Liberty Guard Station. Watch for sign. Liberty townsite in 2 miles. A national historic site.

Quaint houses on the north side of the single Liberty street belie the destruction of terrain on the south. Heaps of tailings often hide machinery that make them. Mining operation is all on private land and posted, so get your glimpses and do your cursing from the public street.

PROSPECTOR DRIVES

For glimpses of how mining used to be, explore the mining roads east, north, and south of Liberty. Old cabins still dot hillsides. Grown-over heaps of dirt attest to failures and probably a few modest successes. Some claims are still active.

REDTOP MOUNTAIN

A prime agate-hunting area but a fine view spot too.

From Highway 97, turn west up road No. 2106 beyond the Mineral Springs Resort and just across the Blue Creek bridge. Follow signs. Park up a spur marked "Agate Bed Parking."

To reach the lookout—with views of Rainier, Stuart, the tip of Adams, other peaks in the Cascades, and Ellensburg and Cle Elum valleys—take trail from the parking area. Trail climbs the west side of the mountain across steep meadows.

Return on a trail that heads north from the lookout and then creeps around a steep bluff to the meadow trail system.

To reach the open agate meadows, which look like they had just undergone a shattering artillery barrage, follow signs beyond the parking area, hiking as far as you like. Spurs lead to Blue Creek Spring and other digging areas.

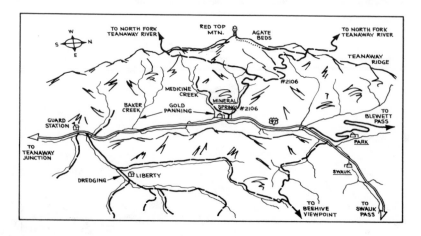

The "battlefield"—school children digging for agates on Redtop Mountain

GOLD PANNING

As always, no promises. But gold is still being mined and panned in this area. Favorite creeks include Medicine Creek above the Mineral Springs Campground, Baker Creek above the Baker Campground, and all creeks in the Liberty area.

One warning. Some of the creeks may cross private land. Some may be part of patented mining claims. If posted, don't trespass.

59   BLEWETT PASS

Leaf fossils and history along an abandoned section of state highway that became so much a part of the state's transportation history that the new pass (the Swauk) still is called by the old name.

From Seattle, turn off I-90 at the Wenatchee Interchange east of Cle Elum, continuing north on Highway 97 to Swauk Pass (still called Blewett Pass on some highway reports) in 24 miles.

The old highway often is not free of snow until mid-June.

OLD BLEWETT PASS HIGHWAY

For an interesting respite from the usual freeway straightaway rush, drive a mountain highway built as highways used to be, full of curves, twists, and hairpin turns. One-way traffic in some places.

Turn left (north) off Highway 97 about 16.5 miles from the Wenatchee Interchange. The old highway—now forest road No. 2208—twists to the old pass at 4064 feet and then snakes its way down to the new highway about 2 miles south of the old Blewett townsite. An 11-mile trip.

Occasional views and signs of old mining operations mark the trip. Heaviest mining near the summit.

LEAF FOSSILS

Find fossils and leaf imprints of plants that grew when the climate here was almost tropical.

Watch for dark bands in road-cut rock ½ mile west of Swauk Pass on Highway 97. Dark bands contain coal-like fossils. Imprints are found in sandstone bordering the bands.

BLEWETT TOWNSITE

A tumbledown mining mill and an ore-grinding stone (arrastra) carved in solid rock are all that remain today of a mining town that boomed in the late 1800s.

Drive 10½ miles north of Swauk Pass on Highway 97.

Look on the west side of the road for the collapsing mill where gold was once processed. Gold was taken from mines in Culver Gulch behind the mill.

The arrastra—base of a water-powered ore-grinding machine—is located to the east of the highway over a bank several hundred yards south of the building.

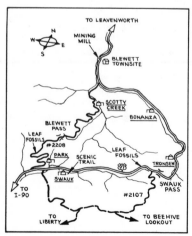

Old (and dangerous) mine shaft near Blewett townsite

SCULPTURE ROCK TRAIL

Geology of the Swauk area unfolds on an easy ¾-mile nature trail out of the Swauk Campground.

Trail starts at the picnic shelter, crosses Swauk Creek, and then turns east, winding back to the far end of the campground.

The pathway loops around sandstone and basalt outcrops, past viewpoints and through timber typical of the entire area.

60   LION ROCK

Leave the valley to enjoy the brisk silence of alpine meadows and ridge tops—all bursting with views.

Drive north on Highway 97 from the Wenatchee Interchange to Swauk Pass, 24 miles, turning right (south) on forest road No. 2107 just below the summit. Roads in this area are narrow with few turnouts and tend to get slippery and greasy after rains. But views from all of them are spectacular.

Snow may block some roads until July.

LION ROCK VIEW

A lonesome view out over the Swauk valley to the Enchantment Peaks, Stuart, and Mt. Rainier. At night listen for coyotes in the valley.

From Swauk Pass follow road No. 2107 along Swauk Ridge to a junction with road No. 2100 to the south. Turnoff to the viewpoint on road No. 2008 in 4 miles. This road may be extremely rough for it is almost never maintained.

From Ellensburg, drive north on the Green Canyon road off Highway 97, less than 2 miles from Ellensburg toward Virden. Follow road to the Reece Canyon road continuing uphill to the top of the plateau. Watch for campground signs. A smoother route.

Camp either at the campground away from the edge of Table Mountain or at any of many undeveloped open areas on the mountain's rim. (Carry water.) You may find a cow bawling at your tent door in the morning. Grazing is permitted. Agates and Indian artifacts are sometimes found in this area.

For a walk-in view, hike north ¼ mile from the junction of Lion Rock Lookout

road and road No. 2100. Follow a jeep track to start and then walk west to the edge of the ridge and make your way across open slopes uphill as far as you want.

DEVILS GULCH

Drive through high meadows to look down on the stark eroded-sandstone slab-sides of Devils Gulch.

Continue on road No. 2107 from Swauk Pass, pass the Lion Rock junction, driving first through Haney Meadows (watch for cabins and a fenced area) and then to the rim of the gulch at between 5800 and 6000 feet.

Views over the gulch to the north from occasional turnouts or stop almost anywhere along the high road and walk to the sharp canyon lip for a new view. Glimpses of Stuart over lupines on some turns.

(This road gets rougher and rougher every year. The Forest Service does prac-tically nothing to either maintain it or control wet-weather spring and fall use which causes all the deep ruts. In the Forest Service view, the road "serves no pur-pose"—meaning, of course, that it makes no money and that recreation, really, isn't a Forest Service purpose. You judge—and write.)

MISSION PEAK

Hike up an abandoned road to one of the highest and best views in this area. See not only Rainier and Stuart but Glacier, Baker, Wenatchee, and Rocky Reach Dam on the Columbia River.

Watch for a road spur on the south side of road No. 2100 east of Devils Gulch shortly after the road turns northerly. At one time you could drive to a small lake at 6100 feet. But you shouldn't try it now. The road, like so many on these high ridges, is not maintained because, of course, there's no money being made on logging here at the moment.

Walk up the road to the lake and then another ¾ mile to a long-abandoned lookout site at 6878 feet. (And try to come to some judgment en route as to who is serving who in the public forests.)

BEEHIVE

Look down on Wenatchee, up the Columbia Gorge toward Chelan, south to the Mission Ridge ski area, and out at Stuart and the Cascades.

Drive about 22½ miles from Swauk Pass, past Devils Gulch to a turnoff leading to a former lookout site at 4576 feet. Watch for sign.

A private-seeming site when seen from the lip of Devil's Gulch. But definitely a wide-open view once you arrive. Road may be extremely rough. It is seldom maintained.

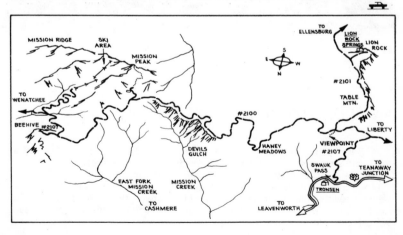

Esmeralda Peaks and North Fork Teanaway River Road

AA   NORTH FORK TEANAWAY RIVER

A river that barely trickles across farm land in Swauk Prairie roars like a mountain stream should nearer its source. Irrigators drain most of the river at lower levels but have no effect on the river higher up.

From Seattle, drive east over Snoqualmie Pass, turning off I-90 at the Wenatchee Interchange No. 85 east of Cle Elum, driving north on Highway 97. To reach the Teanaway River turn left (north) off 97 in about 6 miles on county road 9221. Follow North Fork signs.

CAMPGROUNDS
Beverly—13 sites in pleasant open wooded area along the river. Most sites oriented to the river. 17 miles from Highway 97. Pit toilets.
DeRoux—2 sites near the river. An undeveloped camp in open timber. Pit toilets. 20 miles from Highway 97.

Undeveloped sites are to be found all along the river and off logging spurs. Find your own. Some are very nice.

61 TEANAWAY

From the Wenatchee Junction east of Cle Elum drive 6 miles north on Highway 97, turning left onto the Teanaway River road, bearing north in about 7 miles onto the North Fork road.

REDTOP LOOP
Drive up one road and back another for views from the lookout and meadows on Redtop Mountain. (See the Swauk)
Turn east off the river road just beyond the timber company campground at Dickey Creek. Watch for lookout turnout to the north at the top of the ridge.
To return via Jack Creek road, continue east to junction with road No. 2106, turning left to reach the Teanaway. Road to the right leads to Highway 97 near Mineral Springs.
Total loop about 21 miles.

STAFFORD VIEWPOINT
See Rainier, Ingalls Peak, and open meadows of the Teanaway River valley from a former lookout site at 3784 feet.
Turn east off the river road onto the Stafford Creek road No. 2226 less than 2½ miles south of Beverly Campground. In less than a mile turn north on road No. 2210. Lookout in 2 miles. Road can be narrow and rough. Park at road end and climb a short switchback trail to former tower site.

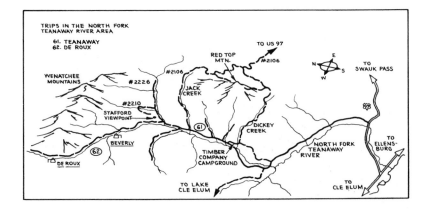

62 DE ROUX

Spring waits here until mid-July some years. Roads often plugged with snow until then.

From Seattle, drive east over Snoqualmie Pass, turning off I-90 at the Wenatchee Interchange east of Cle Elum. Continue east on Highway 97, turning left (north) in about 6 miles onto the Teanaway River Road. DeRoux Campground in about 20 miles.

TEANAWAY FALLS

A rock-shredded torrent at high water dwindles to no more than a busy cascade in late summer.

Drive to the end of the North Fork Teanaway road, about 22 miles from the junction with Highway 97. Small parking area at the road end.

A trail alongside the falls leads to alpine meadows within ¼ mile. Trail continues up the valley another 2 miles to more meadows, old cabins, and diggings.

Falls can be seen at high water from the parking area. Better views, however, closeup. Watch for goats on surrounding rock ledges and early in the year note other cascades pouring out of high valleys.

From the trail, look up at Esmeralda Peaks and the Wenatchee Mountains. Find gentian, paintbrush, and fringed parnassus on the meadows even during the driest autumns. A climbing route to Mount Stuart and Ingalls Peak.

In ¾ mile, trail forks right to Long's Pass and Ingalls Lake.

BEVERLY CREEK TRAIL

Gnarled alpine larch, hundreds of years old, in an open subalpine basin on upper Beverly Creek. A 2-mile hike.

Turn right (east) off the river road just south of the Beverly Campground. Find the trail at the end of a logging spur in less than 2 miles.

Trail climbs to timberline in about 1½ miles. Some of stunted larch and Douglas fir, big at the base but much shorter than their lower-valley counterparts, may be as much as 600 years old. Trail continues over the crest of the Wenatchee Mountain ridge into Ingalls Creek. The route, a cattle driveway to alpine pastures, is also used to reach Mount Stuart.

DE ROUX CREEK TRAIL

A pleasant walk through open timber along a busy stream to series of small waterfalls.

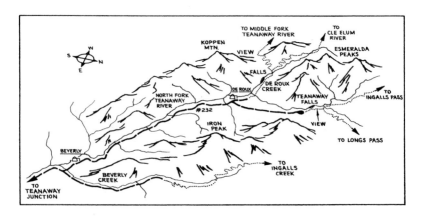

Fireweed

Watch for a road spur to the west just north of the DeRoux Campground. Follow the spur downhill, past several primitive camp spots, driving as far as you can.

Find the trail off fire road around the bottom edge of the clear cut. Trail fords the river and follows the north side of the creek.

A series of waterfalls in 1½ miles. For views, climb a very steep trail of less than ½ mile to the ridge above the Middle Fork. Watch for spur-trail sign. Main trail continues about 3½ miles to Gallagher Head Lake in meadows between Hawkins Mountain and Esmeralda Peaks.

BB   TANEUM (tay'num)

Ridge trails, high meadows, and lookout views from an area not as heavily used as most.

From Seattle, drive beyond Cle Elum toward Ellensburg turning off at the Elk Heights Interchange No. 93 just beyond the rest area. Watch for Taneum Creek signs. Follow Taneum signs.

Or, turn off at Cle Elum interchange No. 84, crossing under the freeway on Fourth Street (before the exit road reaches the downtown section). Continue south and follow road No. 1903 as it winds first to the east and then uphill to the complex of Taneum area roads. Not for trailers.

CAMPGROUNDS

Taneum—12 campsites. 16 picnic units in open timber area on Taneum Creek. Some sites oriented to the river. 11 miles from U.S. 10. Pit toilets. Piped water. Federal fee.

Tamarack Springs—3 sites in a corral near a boxed spring. Pit toilet.

Quartz Spring—3 sites in wooded area just below Quartz Mountain. Water. Pit toilets.

Buck Meadows—6 units near creek. Pit toilets.

Undeveloped camping spots available along most roads in the Gnat Flat-to-Quartz Mountain area.

63   TANEUM CREEK

"A WHITE WOMAN'S GRAVE"

A grave heaped with rock and surrounded by a wooden fence marks a tragedy of the pioneer past.

Find the grave about 75 yards from the road east of the Tamarack Spring Campground, just across the cattleguard.

A woman who died in childbirth in the mid-1880s while traveling with her family through the mountains by wagon train was buried here. A marking states simply that it is "A White Woman's Grave."

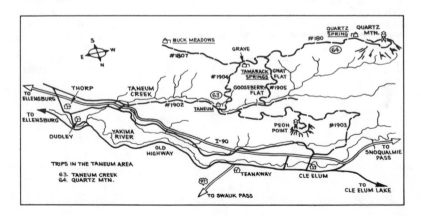

GNAT AND GOOSEBERRY FLATS

In early July, meadows of hyacinths, wild onion, and larkspur beneath slimpses of Rainier, Adams, and Stuart.

From Taneum Campground drive east on road No. 1902, turning south in about 2½ miles on road No. 1905. Views and meadows mix as the road climbs first through Gooseberry and then Gnat Flats.

Continue to Quartz Mountain or return via road No. 1904 and Tamarack Springs.

PEOH POINT

Airplane views of Cle Elum from a lookout 2000 feet above the city and only 2 air-miles away.

Either drive south from Cle Elum on road No. 1903 (see above) or west from Taneum Campground on roads No. 1902 and 1902C. At the junction of the two atop the ridge either proceed north on a very narrow and rough road to the lookout. Or—better yet—turn eastward on 1903 taking a better developed logging road No. 1903B to the north in a little more than a half-mile at a 4-way intersection.

Excellent views not only of Cle Elum but of the Yakima River valley, Lake Cle Elum, and the Cle Elum River drainage. To drive to Cle Elum take road No. 1903 downhill, following signs. 🚗

"A white woman's grave" on Taneum River Road

Dutch Miller Peaks from Quartz Mountain

64   QUARTZ MOUNTAIN

Drive through high meadows to ridge trails and awesome mountain views.

From Taneum Campground (see page 36) continue west on road No. 1902, turning south on No. 1905 in about 2½ miles. Follow signs to the former lookout site at the end of road No. 1935F. Total distance. 18 miles.

QUARTZ MOUNTAIN VIEWPOINT

Peaks spread from Mt. Adams to Glacier during the day. At sunset, watch elk on lower meadows and at night, stars so thick you can't believe it.

If snow blocks the steep road to the bench where the tower used to be, park in a meadow and hike up.

From edge of the bench see Rainier, Stuart, and the Cascades in addition to Adams and Glacier. A small, open meadow just north of the tower site provides an ideal spot for star and elk watching.

PEACHES RIDGE

A very nice name for a very nice place.

Watch for a trail off the last sharp turn on the road to Quartz Mountain lookout site. Drop down the Manastash Ridge trail to Peaches Ridge trail junction in about ½ mile.

With Mount Rainier over your left shoulder walk out high meadows with views down the Yakima River valley and glimpses of the red barns near Ellensburg. Walk a mile or more. Trail drops into heavier timber the farther it goes.

TANEUM LAKE

A level trail leads to a small, pretty mountain lake nestled in timber. ¾ mile.

Watch for trail sign and small parking spot on north side of the road about 3 miles east of Quartz Mountain Lookout.

A primitive camping spot near the trail at the lake. Trails also loop the lake. Watch for blue anemone and clematis. No scooters, or horses.

FROST MOUNTAIN

Hike 1½ miles through timbered hills for views of Rainier, Cle Elum Lake, and the Stuart Range with deer and elk added in the evening and morning.

Find lookout sign on the north side of road No. 180 about 1½ miles west of the junction with No. 1904.

Follow a steep path to the first bench above the road, then a trail that alternately crosses flat meadows and climbs steep slopes to the lookout at 5740 feet. Tower is manned during the fire season.

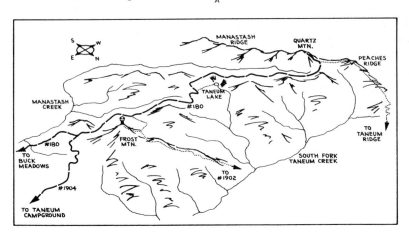

Family hike

CC   STAMPEDE PASS

1000 acres of huckleberries and mile-squares of logged-off private land, criss-crossed by powerlines and construction roads, topped with a weather station.

Take the Kachess Lake-Stampede Pass turn-off on I-90 (exit No. 62) about 2 miles beyond the end of Keechelus Lake. Keep right on road No. 212. In 5 miles, turn left at Lizard Lake on road No. 2190A, following the yellow targets to the weather station complex.

West end of the Green River Road is blocked by City of Tacoma watershed gates.

The **weather station,** only one in the state atop the Cascade Crest, keeps tab 24 hours a day on shifting mountain weather, supplying information to other weather stations and passing airplanes.

The station's crew, snowbound in winter, welcomes visitors anytime. Equipment, which men on duty are glad to explain, ranges from a special scale for weighing the amount of moisture in wood—part of a procedure for rating forest fire danger—to exotic electronic gear for receiving and transmitting information on winds, temperatures, pressures, humidity, etc.

From a former lookout site nearby find views of Lake Kachess, Mount Rainier, Mount Daniel, and the Yakima River and Cedar River valleys.

The concrete pads below the lookout site were once used as missile-test launching pads by The Boeing Co.

CASCADE CREST TRAIL

Hike north or south along the Cascade Crest Trail for continuing new views of both the eastern and western slopes of the Cascades.

Find trail to the north near Lizard Lake at Stampede Pass (see above). Trail winds toward Dandy Pass in less than 2 miles.

To hike south, pick up trail at the weather station, hiking out ridges for continuing views. Snowshoe Butte in 5 miles.

CAMPGROUNDS

Crystal Springs—20 units stretched out along the Yakima River. Most near the river. Timbered area closer to U.S. 10 than it seems. Some highway noise. Pit toilets. Turn right at Stampede Pass turnoff. Charge.

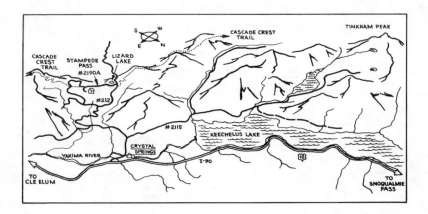

DD   KACHESS AND CLE ELUM LAKES

The two lakes are among the most heavily used recreation areas east of the Cascades. Both are within the Cle Elum Ranger District of Wenatchee National Forest. District headquarters are in Cle Elum.

To reach the lakes drive east from Seattle on I-90 over Snoqualmie Pass. Turn off to Kachess Lake at the Kachess Lake-Stampede Pass signs. To reach Cle Elum Lake, leave the freeway at Cle Elum or at the Salmon la Sac overpass 3 miles west of Cle Elum and follow signs through the mining towns of Roslyn and Ronald.

CAMPGROUNDS

Kachess—180 units, including 26 trailer-only sites. Located in a timbered peninsula between Kachess and Little Kachess Lakes. Some sites near the lakes, others on Gale Creek. Swimming. Boat launching. Piped water. Restrooms. Charge.

Wishpoosh—39 sites on Cle Elum Lake 10 miles north of Cle Elum. Boat-launch, and picnic facility. Family sites. Toilets. Water. Charge.

Cooper Lake

Cle Elum River—17 tables in open timber near the Cle Elum river 15 miles from Cle Elum. Pit toilets.

Red Mountain—13 sites along the river. Entrance road not recommended for trailers. Pit toilets.

Owhi Camp—20 walk-in tent sites on Cooper Lake. All oriented to the lake. No motors on lake. Pit toilets.

Salmon la Sac—110 sites at the juncture of the Cle Elum and Cooper Rivers. Most sites oriented to one of the rivers. A heavy-use area. Piped water. Flush toilets. Charge.

Fish Lake—10 sites near the Fish Lake Guard Station. Not recommended for trailers. Pit toilets.

Tacquala Meadows—9 sites along the river at the end of the road. Pit toilets.

Others—Undeveloped camping areas can be found all along the Cle Elum River from the lake to the end of the road at the trailhead to Hyas Lake. Tables have been placed in some areas. Most, however, consist simply of an open spot on a river bank.

Calypso orchid (fairy slipper) blooming in May in the Salmon la Sac Campground

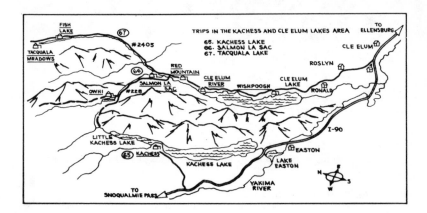

Boating on Little Kachess Lake

65   KACHESS LAKE

Drive east from Seattle over Snoqualmie Pass on I-90. Turn off at the Stampede Pass-Kachess Lake sign and follow signs 5 miles to the Kachess Campground.

WATERFALLS AND BOX RIDGE VIEWS
Just 5 miles to views of the Cascades and out over Kachess Lake with waterfalls along the way. Lots of color in the fall.

Take road No. 2214 up Box Canyon Creek at the campground entrance junction. (Turn left at the "T" intersection if driving directly from Seattle.)

Waterfalls to the right in Box Canyon Creek in the first mile. Watch for flashes of white water through the trees. Stop and explore on your own.

Views of Mount Margaret (5500) over Box Canyon Creek, then over the lake before the road loops west again for views of Alta Mountain (6144) and other Cascade peaks from about 3900 feet.

LITTLE KACHESS TRAIL

An easy wooded walk above Little Kachess Lake with a view of a small island in 2 miles.

Find trail at the upper end of Kachess Campground. If you camp, follow unmarked trails through camp and along the lakeshore to the trailhead. The trail continues to the end of the lake in about 5 miles, forking left up Mineral Creek less than a mile beyond the lake toward Cooper Pass.

BIG TREE NATURE TRAIL

A ½-mile loop through an old-growth stand of Douglas fir, some measuring 7 ½ feet in diameter. Fifteen signs describe the succession of plants in a forest and the inter-relationship of plants, animals, insects, and man in the evolution of forest life.

Trail begins at campground entrance. Watch for sign.

MUSHROOMS AND COLOR

Find both mushrooms and the brilliant reds of Douglas maple along Gale Creek road No. 2213.

Turn left off road No. 2214 (road to Box Ridge) in less than a mile from the "T" junction west of the campground.

Color in clear cuts. Most mushrooms in old-growth timber. Search out your own.

At the road end, hike left up an old bulldozer trace to Swan Lake (below the track) and Rock Rabbit Lake (at the end). Both in less than ½ mile. Both are fishing lakes but still interesting spots to explore.

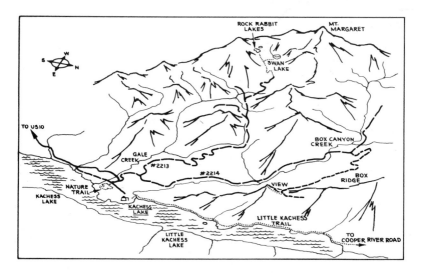

66   SALMON LA SAC

Drive east from Seattle over Snoqualmie Pass on I-90. Turn off at Salmon la Sac Interchange No. 80 or at Cle Elum. In Cle Elum follow signs to Roslyn and Ronald, old coal mining towns, and then on to Salmon la Sac, in 19 miles from Cle Elum.

Salmon la Sac was named by Frenchmen who saw Indians netting salmon in rapids below the bridge in cedar bark (sack) baskets. Dams have long since ended the salmon runs.

COOPER PASS

An easy road to high views out of Salmon la Sac.

Turn west onto road No. 228 off the Cle Elum River road about a mile south of the Salmon la Sac Guard Station. Follow the road uphill past Cooper Lake to a pass with vistas over Kachess Lake and out to peaks of the Cascade Crest.

(The road continues over the pass almost down to Kachess Lake. Conservationists hope it will never go any farther, but . . . .) ⭆

COOPER LAKE

A prime recreation area that's still in a state of flux. Recreationists feel strongly that it ought to be kept as the wild place it really is. But developers, loggers and others have other ideas.

From the Cooper Pass road (see above) turn right onto road to Cooper Lake. Find Owhi Campground across the bridge to the left. A walk-in camp. No motors permitted on the lake. ⭆

PETE LAKE TRAIL

Snow patched ridges circle a rock-filled lake that hints of all of the beauties to be found at lakes still farther on.

At the campground junction (see above) continue straight ahead on logging road No. 235 to the end of the road. Trail leaves the road-end, crosses a clear cut and then drops downhill into lovely forest to join the old Cooper Lake-Pete Lake trail. Follow the old trail uphill to the lake. An easy and pleasant walk. 2½ miles.

Viewpoints at the lake near the outlet and from rocky ridges above the trail on the way to a shelter. Lots of picnic and camping spots. Paths continue on to Spectacle and Escondido lakes.

You can also hike to the lake on a 4-mile trail from Cooper Lake. Originally, the forest service promised to close the logging road and maintain only the longer trail. But you can see what happened! 🚶

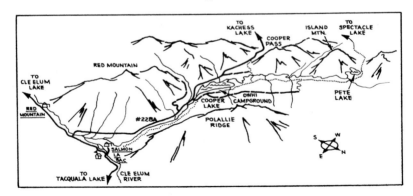

Left to right: Lemah Mountain, Chimney Rock, Overcoat Peak, and Summit Chief from Cooper River Road

COOPER RIVER TRAIL
Walk 4 miles, generally downhill, along the Cooper River from Cooper Lake to the Salmon la Sac Campground.

Find the trail on the north side of the river off the road to the Owhi Campground on Cooper Lake. A good walk home after a visit to the lake or the pass.

ARTIFACTS AND DRIFTWOOD
Find driftwood along the shore and Indian artifacts at low water along Cle Elum Lake.

Artifacts have been found during stump-removal operations on the lake between Bear Creek and Newport Creek. Pick your own.

The driftwood doesn't match the heaps found along the Pacific Ocean. But collectors seeking intimate bits of bleached and gnarled wood for flower decorations and the like will find what they need.

VIEW DRIVE
Turn right off the county road along the east side of Cle Elum Lake about ¼ mile north of Driftwood Acres. Follow road No. 2108 for ½ mile, continuing straight ahead on road No. 2110.

Views over the lake and up the river valley from switchbacks on road No. 2110. Best view from the third switchback in less than 1½ miles.

67   LAKE TACQUALA

Some still call this area "Fish Lake." But the beautiful place deserves its Indian name of Tacquala.

From Seattle drive over Snoqualmie Pass on I-90, turning off either at Salmon la Sac interchange or at Cle Elum. From Cle Elum follow signs to Roslyn and past Salmon la Sac, about 29 miles to meadows at 3400 feet.

HYAS LAKE

An extremely popular 1½-mile walk for two very simple reasons: It's easy and it's scenic.

Drive to the end of the Cle Elum River road No. 2405, about 2 miles beyond the Fish Lake Guard Station. Parking area and campground at the end of the road.

Trail wanders through timber and along the edge of an occasional meadow to a pretty lake nested below Cathedral Rock and Mount Daniel. Camp spots in timber just before the trail reaches the lake. Other campsites along the lake and at the upper end.

Tacquala (Fish) Lake and Cathedral Rock

Best views from open slopes at the upper end of the lake. Trail continues on to Deception Pass, a steady climb of another 2 miles from the upper end of the lake.

LAKE TACQUALA
A long string of water, bordered by flower meadows, that flows like a river in spots.

Drive 10.1 miles beyond the Salmon la Sac Guard Station. Formal camping spots at the southern end of the lake.

A beautiful place to explore by canoe. Paddle from the lower end of the lake up the deep river-like channel to wider shallows in about 2 miles. Or explore the flat marshy lower end of the lake. Meadows along the east side of the lake bloom full of shooting stars in the spring.

Uplake views of Cathedral Rock.

SALMON LA SAC TO TACQUALA LAKE
Vignettes of Indian and mining history along the road from Salmon la Sac to the Fish Lake Guard Station. 11.2 miles.

China Point—Legend has it that during the heyday of mining in the Deception Pass area above Hyas Lake, murdered Chinese were dropped over the cliff into the river. 1.2 miles from Salmon la Sac Guard Station.

Indian Camp—Open meadows on both sides of the road 8.7 miles from Salmon la Sac were once favorite camping grounds for Indians in the valley. Occasional artifacts are still found in the area.

Stage Depot—The log cabin guard station at Salmon la Sac originally served as a depot for a stage line that operated up the valley during mining days.

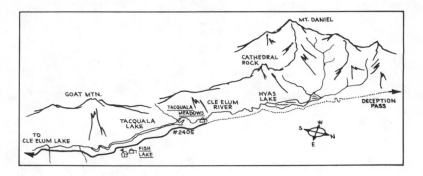

From Lookout Mountain near Twisp

OBTAINING INFORMATION
AND MAPS

Information on the condition of roads and trails can be obtained at the following headquarter and district offices of the Forest Service and National Park Service.

Maps can be obtained at ranger stations or by writing headquarter offices.

WENATCHEE NATIONAL FOREST
Headquarters, P.O. Box 811, Wenatchee, Wash. 98801.
Lake Wenatchee Ranger Station, Star Route, Leavenworth, Wash. 98826.
Leavenworth Ranger Station, Leavenworth, Wash. 98826.
Entiat Ranger Station, Entiat, Wash. 98822.
Chelan Ranger Station, Chelan, Wash. 98816.
Lake Wenatchee Ranger Station, Star Route, Leavenworth, Wash. 98826.
Leavenworth Ranger Station, Leavenworth, Wash. 98826.

OKANOGAN NATIONAL FOREST
Headquarters, Box 950, Okanogan, Wash. 98840.

MOUNT BAKER—SNOQUALMIE NATIONAL FOREST
Headquarters, 1601 2nd Ave., Seattle, Wash. 98101.
Glacier Ranger Station, Glacier, Wash. 98244.
Baker River Ranger Station, Concrete, Wash. 98237.
Darrington Ranger Station, Darrington, Wash. 98241.
Verlot Ranger Station, Granite Falls, Wash. 98252.
Skykomish Ranger Station, Skykomish, Wash. 98288.
North Bend Ranger Station, North Bend, Wash. 98045.

NORTH CASCADES NATIONAL PARK
Headquarters, 311 State Street, Sedro Woolley, Wash. 98284.

READING SUGGESTIONS

Readers may find the following books helpful in gaining a fuller understanding of the outdoors.

Trees, Flowers
Trees, Shrubs and Flowers to Know in Washington, C.P. Lyon. J.M. Dent and Sons, Ltd. Vancouver, B.C., Canada; 1956.
101 Wildflowers of Olympic National Park, Grant and Wenonah Sharpe. University of Washington Press. Seattle; 1957.
Vascular Plants of the Pacific Northwest, Hitchcock, Cronquist, Owenby and Thompson. 5 vols. University of Washington Press. Seattle; 1959.
Northwest Trees, Stephen F. Arno and Ramona P. Hammerly. The Mountaineers. Seattle; 1977.
Plants and Animals of the Pacific Northwest, Eugene N. Kozloff. University of Washington Press. Seattle; 1976.

Seashore
The Edge of the Sea, Rachel Carson. Houghton Mifflin and Co. Boston; 1955.
The Olympic Seashore, Ruth Kirk. Olympic Natural History Association. Port Angeles, Wash.; 1962.
Between Pacific Tides, Edward Rickets and Jack Calvin. Stanford University Press. Palo Alto, Calif.; 1948.
Animals of the Seashore, Muriel Guberlet. Binfords and Mort. Portland, Ore.; 1936.
Seaweeds at Ebbtide, Muriel Guberlet. University of Washington Press. Seattle; 1956.
Common Seaweeds of the Pacific Coast, J. Robert Waaland. Pacific Search Press. Seattle; 1977.
Living Shores of the Pacific Northwest, Lynwood Smith and Bernard Nist. Pacific Search Press. Seattle; 1976.

Nature Guides
A Field Guide to Western Birds, Roger Tory Peterson. Houghton Mifflin Company. Boston.
A Field Guide to the Mammals, William H. Burt and Richard P. Grossenheider. Houghton Mifflin Company. Boston.
A Field Guide to Animal Tracks, Olaus J. Murie. Houghton Mifflin Company. Boston.
A Field Guide to the Ferns, Boughton Cobb. Houghton Mifflin Company, Boston.
A Field Book of Nature Activities and Conservation, William Hillcourt. Putnam and Sons. New York; 1961.
Insects, Ross E. Hutchins. Prentice-Hall, Inc. Englewood Cliffs, N.J.; 1966.
Butterflies Afield in the Pacific Northwest, William Neill and Douglas Hepburn. Pacific Search Press. Seattle; 1976.
Little Mammals of the Pacific Northwest, Ellen Kritzman. Pacific Search Press. Seattle; 1976.
The Audubon Society Field Guide to North American Birds: Western Region Guide, M.F.D. Udvardy. Alfred A. Knopf; 1977.

Geology
Scenic Geology of the Pacific Northwest, Leonard C. Ekman. Binfords and Mort. Portland, Ore.; 1962.
Principles of Geology, James Gilluly, A.C. Waters and A.O. Woodford. W.H. Freeman and Co., San Francisco; 1951.

Origin of Cascade Landscapes, J. Hoover Mackin and Allen S. Cares. Div. Mines and Geology Ind. Circ. No. 41, Washington State Department of Conservation; 1965.

Routes and Rocks, Hiker's Guide to the North Cascades from Glacier Peak to Lake Chelan, D.F. Crowder and R.W. Tabor. The Mountaineers. Seattle; 1965. (Out of print)

Elements of Geology, James H. Zumberge. John Wiley and Sons, Inc. New York; 1959.

Fire and Ice, Stephen L. Harris. The Mountaineers and Pacific Search Press. Seattle; 1976.

Cascadia: The Geologic Evolution of the Pacific Northwest, Bates McKee. McGraw-Hill Book Company; 1972.

Mushrooms

The Savory Wild Mushroom, Margaret McKenny. University of Washington Press. Seattle; 1962.

Mushroom Hunter's Field Guide, Alexander H. Smith. University of Michigan Press. Ann Arbor, Mich.; 1958.

Wilderness Travel

Mountaineering, The Freedom of the Hills, The Mountaineers. Seattle.

Going Light with Backpack or Burro, David Brower, ed. The Sierra Club. San Francisco; 1958.

Backpacking: One Step at a Time, Harvey Manning. The REI Press. Seattle; 1972.

Conservation

Wild Cascades: Forgotten Parkland, Harvey Manning. The Sierra Club. San Francisco; 1965.

My Wilderness: The Pacific West, William O. Douglas. Doubleday and Company, Inc. Garden City, N.Y.; 1960.

A Sand County Almanac, Aldo Leopold. Oxford University Press. New York; 1949.

Steep Trails, John Muir. Houghton Mifflin Company. New York; 1918.

Guides

Cascade Alpine Guide: Climbing and High Routes; Columbia River to Stevens Pass (1973), **Stevens Pass to Rainy Pass** (1977), Fred Beckey. The Mountaineers. Seattle.

The Alpine Lakes, Ed Cooper, Bob Gunning and Brock Evans. The Mountaineers. Seattle; 1971. (Out of print)

BOOKS FROM THE MOUNTAINEERS

50 Hikes in Mount Rainier National Park
101 Hikes in the North Cascades
102 Hikes in the Alpine Lakes, South Cascades and Olympics
103 Hikes in Southwestern British Columbia
109 Walks in B.C.'s Lower Mainland
Trips and Trails, 1: Family Camps, Short Hikes and View Roads around the
    North Cascades
Trips and Trails, 2: Family Camps, Short Hikes and View Roads in the Olympics,
    Mount Rainier and South Cascades
Bicycling the Backroads Around Puget Sound
Bicycling the Backroads of Northwest Washington
Discover Southeast Alaska with Pack and Paddle
55 Ways to the Wilderness in Southcentral Alaska
Footsore 1: Walks and Hikes Around Puget Sound
Footsore 2: Walks and Hikes Around Puget Sound
Hikers' Map to the North Cascades: Routes and Rocks in the Mt.
    Challenger Quadrangle
Hikers'/Climbers' Maps of Glacier Peak and Monte Cristo
Guide to Leavenworth Rock Climbing Areas
Cascade Alpine Guide: Climbing and High Routes, Columbia River to Stevens Pass
Cascade Alpine Guide: Climbing and High Routes, Stevens Pass to Rainy Pass
Climbers' Guide to the Olympic Mountains
Darrington and Index: Rock Climbing Guide
Snow Trails: Ski and Snowshoe Routes in the Cascades
Showshoeing
Mountaineering: The Freedom of the Hills
Medicine for Mountaineering
Mountaineering First Aid
The South Cascades: The Gifford Pinchot National Forest
Challenge of Mount Rainier
The Unknown Mountain
Fire and Ice: The Cascade Volcanoes
Across the Olympic Mountains: The Press Expedition
Men, Mules and Mountains: Lieutenant O'Neil's Olympic Expeditions
The Coffee Chased Us Up: Monte Cristo Memories
Challenge of the North Cascades
Bicycling Notes
Hiking Notes
Climbing Notes
Mountains of the World
The Mountaineer
Northwest Trees
The Ascent of Denali
Storm and Sorrow in the High Pamirs
Canoe Routes: Yukon Territory
Canoe Routes: British Columbia